A GPS for the Spirit

Recalculating Your Spiritual Direction

J. R. Damiani

Published by Frontline Press
P.O. Box 764499
Dallas, TX 75376

Printed in the United States of America

ISBN 978-14507-0599-8

Unless otherwise indicated, Scripture quotations are from King James Version of the Bible and the New King James Version (NKJV) 1976, J. Thomas Nelson Publishers, Nashville, TN. Quotes from The Living Bible are from Tyndale House Publishers, Wheaton, Illinois, 1971.

Cover artwork by Luke Smarto
Cover design by Keith Bilbrey
First printing April 2010

This book is dedicated to the congregation
of Family Worship Center
for 26 years of faithfulness and friendship.

ACKNOWLEDGEMENTS

I must thank my two mentors, who, without their knowledge, have inspired my life and ministry immensely: the late Dr. C. M. Ward of Revivaltime fame and Pastor Dan Betzer of First Assembly in Fort Myers. Thanks also to Don Smarto for encouragement and his help in editing this devotional.

INTRODUCTION

I have been in public ministry for nearly 50 years, starting as a rookie gospel singer in 1960. Along with some friends in youth group, I organized the Eastmen Quartet and traveled for 20 years with the group and 5 years with my family. After 20 years of "on the job" training, my wife Beverly and I felt called to plant a church, and at 43 years of age, we started Family Worship Center in Lansdale, PA. January 15, 1984, was our start-up date. These devotionals are a result of days and years of research and study. Most of them are condensed from messages that I preached and newspaper articles that I submitted to our local paper. Some have come from my weekly radio program, "The Good News Break"—Sunday mornings at 8:00 a.m. over our local Lansdale station at WNPV 1440 AM.

There's no question about the fact that it's easy to be distracted during your spiritual journey. In Dottie Rambo's song "Just in Time", she included the lyrics, "I don't remember drifting, 'cause pleasure rode with me. When careless winds start blowing, you drift so easily."

This book is designed to kick-start your day or your week with meaningful messages and usable scriptural advice to help you to keep your mind renewed, your spiritual direction clear and to keep you from drifting.

As you read, try not to read it in one sitting, or to study several devotionals at one time. It is designed to be absorbed thoughtfully and with an open heart. Read a chapter in the morning and meditate on it during your day—you may want to read it over again to fully process the message. If some recalculation needs to happen, allow the Spirit of God to give you needed direction.

John 16:13… "He will guide you into all truth."

J.R.

Come and See!

I'm always fascinated when I read the first chapter of John. There's so much that we can apply to today. The all-inclusive verse 12 "as many as receive Him to them He gives the power or the right to become someone!" To become a Son of God! How? Through the New Birth. In verse 29 John the Baptist declares that Jesus is the Perfect Sacrifice for sin. The Lamb of God who takes away sin. In verse 33 John declares that Jesus is the Holy Spirit Baptizer. He will fill your heart to overflowing! It's a great chapter.

Philip in this text is already an evangelist. He met Christ and knew that He was the Promised Messiah—and he couldn't wait to tell somebody. He found his friend Nathaniel, who was a very religious man. He was a man who read the Word on a very regular basis—and one who was truly looking for the Messiah. But not the son of a carpenter from Nazareth—gimme a break, Philip! Your enthusiasm is getting ahead of your knowledge. Nazareth? I don't think so. Nothing good can come out of Nazareth! Philip didn't argue, he just said "Come and see!"

Perhaps one good lesson for us in this remark is this, let's declare the Gospel rather than try to defend it. The Word is Powerful! It's convincing! It holds terror for the Enemy of the Cross. Philip knew that he couldn't convince Nathaniel by going back into the Old Testament prophecies of Isaiah or Jeremiah, but he knew what he knew! Nathaniel was curious enough to follow Philip and see for himself. Nathaniel's doubt vanished like a morning fog when he met Jesus! Nathaniel owed his introduction to Jesus to a friend.

Good friends introduce their friends to Jesus! All of his years of praying for the Messiah to be revealed were rewarded. That day Nathaniel began a trip that was far from boring. Nathaniel *came and saw*. The first answer given to this first New Testament doubter is the only answer needed! Nathaniel was there when Jesus performed his first public miracle—at the wedding in Cana of Galilee. He heard Mary say, "Whatever He asks you to do, do it!" He was there when the nobleman's son was healed, in John 5 when the crippled man was healed, and the man who was born blind was made to see again, when the demoniac of Gadera was set free, when Jesus healed Peter's mother-in-law, when the man with the withered hand stood before Jesus and Jesus said "Stretch forth your hand!" The woman who walked bent over at the waist—who stood and saw Jesus eye to eye! Nathaniel saw the awesome phenomenon of Jesus cleansing leprosy, and the widow's son who was raised from the dead! How about the storm on the Sea of Galilee that Jesus stilled with three words—"Peace Be Still!" Nathaniel, come and see! 5,000 fed with 5 loaves and 2 fish! I wonder how often he said to Philip "Thanks for asking me to come and see!"

The question is still asked today "can any good thing come out of Nazareth? Is it real or is it hope so—or pie in the sky by and by?

Has Christ really changed the world? Is His life really worth considering? Can Jesus really fulfill His Word? Is Hebrews 13:8 true? Is Jesus Christ still the same yesterday, today and forever? Come and See!

When the New Life Gets Old

Some of you can remember very well when you were first saved—when Jesus found you and lifted you out of a horrible pit and set your feet on solid ground. There was a definite difference from your former life. Everything looked better and brighter, you loved everybody—even the cat knew you were different. There was a glow about you! Church became a place where you couldn't wait to go. There was a joy at being alive in Jesus. You loved to pray and worship and read the Bible—and most of all, life had a sense of purpose. When old things passed away, the new things were ordered by the Lord! It was definitely a new life! Then something happened. The new life began to get old. The fire became smoke. The first love and childlike faith disappeared.

What happened? Or, how does it happen? Let me suggest four reasons—or four results of the "new life" getting old. The first thing that goes is joy. You are still doing the right things, but not really trusting. You are going through the motions, but you seem to have to force yourself to function in the new life. It becomes harder and harder to be excited about church, or the things of God. Then, because your joy is gone, your strength gets less and less—and you find yourself losing your spiritual appetite. You don't hunger as much as you did before. It becomes harder and harder for you to pray or study or give or work in the Father's business.

The next thing you lose is your love. More and more you become irritated with other church members and other Christians. Fault finding becomes a normal pattern. Feelings get hurt easily—over nothing. What never bothered you when you first experienced the "new life" now is a major offense. It's easier and easier to do things that you wouldn't think of doing when you first received the "new life". You begin to justify your lack of love, and joy, and hunger, and loss of conviction.

So, what to do about it? Revelation 2:5 gives a formula to a church or an individual that needs to be renewed, "Remember from whence you have fallen, and repent, and do the first works." It's time to rekindle the fire! We need to be reminded why we are serving God and why we are working for Him. Remember—and then repent. There's no short cut. There are no substitutions for repentance. Repentance should be part of our spiritual make up.

Let's put our shoulder to the wheel. Let's "get busy" for God. Let the Holy Spirit do a priority check in your life today.

This old world needs to see revived churches and revived Christians. Put on that Spiritual Armor on a daily basis. Satan will try to defeat you because he knows how precious you are to God. Get renewed today!

How Big Is God?

Has anyone ever discovered how big God really is? The Old Testament history tells us that the Syrians, the Philistines, the Amorites, the Hittites, the Egyptians and others all measured God by their own religious concepts. God cannot be discovered by science, or seminary, or psychology, or even by the Supreme Court. Man's wisdom is only a hindrance to faith. You can't discover God; you must experience Him by Faith.

Your faith must be stronger than the faith of the naturalist; his god is Mother Nature. Your faith must be stronger than the faith of biochemist; his god is the test tube. Your faith must be stronger than the political scientist; his god is the government. It takes a personal experience with God, the Creator, in order to have a clear view of who He is.

Too many people count on lucky pieces, images, candles, beads, and smoke. They think that religious ritual impresses God. They'll give God Easter, Christmas, and maybe Thanksgiving, but *they* can handle the rest of the year themselves.

God must be first—and 24 hours a day! The Old Testament story of Naaman is relevant today. Let's look at it for moment. In 1Kings 5 Naaman said in verse 12, "I will not be clean God's way". In verse 13 his servants gave him wise counsel and in verse 14 it says, "he went down and dipped himself seven times" —not five or six, but seven. Verse 15 states, "and his flesh became as a child". He was made perfectly clean; pure and new. God isn't asking for some great thing, just obedience to Him, and He has a right to that claim. He made me, and He bought me back. I belong to Him.

The story of Naaman teaches us several things. First, doubt will cheat you every time. Unbelief makes you blind to what God can do. Faith is like a pair of binoculars that can show you the future. The sinner, the professor, and the humanist think they are so broadminded, but they are shortsighted. They can't see beyond a few rowdy years. Sinners think that they have found utopia. The drug-filled needle or the line of coke, or the pill that they pop produces the shortest paradise on record—so temporary. The thrill of the dance floor and the sensual stimulation that it produces doesn't last until you need a sleeping pill. Young people are turning away from drugs to alcohol, but the contents of that bottle give a cheap thrill. You'll be staggering before you reach the parking lot. If the sinner thinks that he's broadminded, he needs his eyes examined. Faith gives you insight into the future. If Moses hadn't had this insight he may have been an unknown Pharaoh rotting away under some Egyptian pyramid. He is immortal today because of the binoculars of faith. Hebrews 11, the Hall of Faith, tells us that "he chose rather to suffer affliction with the people of God, than to enjoy the pleasures of sin for a season. Esteeming the reproach of Christ greater riches than the treasures of Egypt for he had respect in the God that had promised eternal rewards!" Sin hinders you, it pulls you toward the gutter, and it narrows your view and binds you. Sin promises you the world and settles for death—for the wages of sin is death! Sin leaves life so empty and unfulfilling. When the pressure comes, then you call for God because there's only emptiness in sin. Sin is boring. Sin is monotonous. Go God's way and you'll experience so much more. God offers unlimited adventure. Put Him first and you'll find life. When you put God first and have faith in Him alone you'll discover what living is all about.

God is bigger than religion, God is bigger than tradition, God is bigger than committees and denominations—and yet He's small enough to be personal. He's in your kitchen, He's in the factory, and God is where people get greasy and dirty.

God is the God of every human sorrow. Unbelief will blind you but faith will lead you out.

A Cure for a Troubled Heart

Heart trouble is a problem that plagues thousands of Americans today. It attacks the young and the old, the rich and the poor and everyone in between; but the heart trouble that Jesus was referring to in John 14:1 is not discovered by x-rays, catheterization, or stress tests. Jesus is talking about Spiritual heart trouble and He's giving His disciples some guidelines that would guarantee a cure for a troubled heart. The time is just hours before the trial and the crucifixion.

This was a hard time for Jesus and His disciples. Judas had just betrayed Jesus and had gone into the night. Jesus has washed the disciples feet in an act of servitude. He called on them to love one another as an example to the world. Peter impulsively said to Jesus, "I will lay down my life for your sake." Jesus foretold that Peter would deny Him three times before morning. No wonder their hearts were troubled. What could Jesus possibly say to these 11 faithful followers? Jesus gave them seven love notes.

Verse 1, the comfort of faith, "Let not your heart be troubled; ye believe in God, believe also in Me". Faith is a sustaining comfort. Believe also in me. How many do you know who say, I believe in God, I believe in a Supreme Being—but that's not enough! "Believe also in Me," Jesus said! That word also leads to Calvary, to the empty tomb, to the mount of ascension and on to the throne of God! Jesus is God in the flesh. It's a record that you can't deny. His presence is a presence that cannot be ignored. That's why the world reacts so violently against Jesus, because His claims to deity have been proven. Lots of good men have died, but they have not risen again! Your faith can rest in Jesus. He keeps His promises!

There's the comfort of hope! Verse 2; "In my Father's house" etc. There's a preview of where we're going to live. That hope brought joy to Jesus, Hebrews 12:2, "The author and finisher of our faith". All we gave Him was a smelly stable, but He's preparing Heaven for us!

The comfort of His return. Verse 3, "If I go, I will come again and receive you unto Myself!" All the scoffers may despise me, and no change around me see, but He tells me that He's coming and that's quite enough for me.

There's comfort in knowing the way! Verse 5, Thomas said, "How can we know the way?" When it comes to knowing the way to Heaven it cannot be misunderstood. Jesus said to Thomas, "I am the Way!" When you're dealing with eternal souls, you can't afford to make a mistake. Jesus is crying out "I am the Way, the Truth and the Life". Go to Jesus—on your knees in prayer. He'll show you the way for He is the way.

There's the comfort in prayer. Songwriters have likened prayer to long distance telephone calls. We have an unlimited calling area—and a limitless credit card. I can call collect any hour day or night. Never underestimate the power of prayer.

Overdosed On Life

Many people today are singing the blues. They walk around with heavy burdens. They are easily overtaken by the cares of this life. They have lost the fizz. Their zest is gone. Their tank is empty. There is no way to avoid the blues, and there is no way to avoid the valley. We all experience valley times, but we don't have to stay there. We can go <u>to</u> the valley and then <u>through</u> the valley. David must have experienced valleys. That's why he could write "in the valley He restoreth my soul." (Psalm 23)

We will have valleys, but today I want to help you to get through the valley. To be restored. That's the secret. Elijah felt that he was the only godly man in his town. He prayed that God would kill him. Charles Wesley, with John, is credited for saving England through the great revival that began under his ministry. He was a great man and a great leader. After his conversion he wrote "O for a thousand tongues to sing my Great Redeemer's praise!" But less than a year later he wrote these words, "O where is the blessedness I knew when I first met the Master?"

Each of us goes through the descent. We go from above the clouds to below the clouds. No one wants to descend. Peter, on the Mount of Transfiguration, didn't want to go back down. There were too many needs down there, too many people with the blues, and too many people running on empty. Listen: Jesus never said that He would deliver us FROM trials. He said that He would deliver us IN the trial. He didn't come to deliver us from dying, but to make us victors over death! He took the stinger out of death. Great men have had valleys and low points. These are things that Satan will continue to throw up to you to condemn you. We all feel it—lonely, insecure, and insignificant. If we concentrate on our surroundings, we can't help but sing the blues. Jesus promised to help us in those times.

At the Meramec Caverns in Missouri, the cave guides always turn the light off for 30 seconds. A little girl cried out "Daddy, I'm afraid!" Dad said, "Honey, don't be afraid. **There's someone here who knows how to turn the lights on."** If you're going through a valley and it's dark, Jesus can turn the lights back on. He's only a prayer away.

Christ's Mission Accomplished

While Jesus hung on the Cross in indescribable agony the Gospel reporters recorded His last words—"Father, forgive them for they know not what they do." (Luke 23:34) "Today you will be with me in paradise." (Luke 23:43) "My God, My God, why hast Thou forsaken me?" (Mark 15:34) "Woman, Behold your son" (John 19:26) " Son, behold your mother." (John 19:27) "It is finished!" (John 19:30) And hell rejoiced. In the regions of the damned there was rejoicing, but there was uneasiness in their rejoicing. There was some discomfort in the High Priest and the religious leaders as well. Mathew 27:62 tells us that the Pharisees went to Pilate and asked for a special guard to secure the tomb because Jesus had said, "I will arise on the third day". So they sealed the tomb and soldiers stood guard. Why? They weren't sure what was finished or if it really was finished. They were unbelievers who "sorta" believed. Satan would have loved to know that Jesus' life was finished—that the Light of the World was extinguished. That was his plan, and for a few short hours on that Friday afternoon the light had gone out. Once again darkness fell on planet earth, but while the light was out some powerful things happened. The veil of the temple was torn open from the top to the bottom indicating it was not done by man but by the Supernatural Power of God. The Mercy Seat where the priest would enter to make sacrifice for the sins of the people was now exposed and open.

The rule of the Law was now finished. No longer would they have to come to Jerusalem carrying or leading the sacrificial animal to atone for their sins. Sin was dealt with. Hebrews 9:26, "He put away sin by the sacrifice of Himself." Because of Calvary sin has no more control or dominion over us. That's good news! Condemnation was finished. There is therefore now no condemnation to whom? "To those who are in Christ Jesus and walk not after the flesh but after the Spirit." Those whose walk matches their talk have been made free form the law of sin and death!

The wall of partition or separation from God is finished. He destroyed it. Broke it down! Remember the ecstatic celebration when the Berlin wall came down? This happened in the spiritual realm at Calvary! The wrath of God is finished. Romans 5:9, "Being justified by His blood we shall be saved from wrath through Him."

The curse is finished. Galatians 3:13-14, "Christ has redeemed us from the curse of the law having become a curse (for us for it is written 'cursed is everyone who hangs on a tree')."

Spiritual death is finished. 2 Timothy 1:10, "Our Savior Jesus Christ has abolished death and brought life and immortality to light through the Gospel." Spiritual death has been replaced by abundant life!

The power of principalities and spiritual forces of evil was finished. Colossians 2:15, "Having disarmed principalities and powers, He made a public spectacle of them, triumphing over them in it." The enemy can go no farther than you allow him. The occult, which is very visible and growing in this day and age, can be stopped by one spirit filled, spirit living, Christ honoring, sold out Christian. The spirit realm is real but the Power of the Resurrection is more real!

Satan's power was finished! Jesus said, "I am come to destroy the works of the devil." Hebrews 2:14, "He came to destroy the one who had the power of death, that is the devil, … and release those who through the fear of death were all their lifetime subject to bondage!"

You do not have to be held in the enemy's grip, bound by his chains. You can be free. You need not live in darkness and chains any longer! He came to set the captive free!

How To Be A Friend Of God

People have attained some pretty high levels of visibility in life. Honors have been awarded to sports figures, entertainers, political leaders, even ministers—and many are well deserved and proper. Think about Michael Jordan, Babe Ruth, Jack Nicklaus, Richard Petty—contests and polls are taken to settle on who is best. Which restaurant? Which chili maker? Who makes the best pizza, etc. and the beat goes on. You can be the chairman of the board, the CEO, President, or King, but no title ever can surpass or equal "Friend of God"! What a unique title for a man to have, but is it exclusive only to Abraham? Can others have it as well? Yes, by all means! In fact, if you don't fall into this category, it is because you don't want to.

Abraham was a man of faith-a man of patience and obedience, but prior to this he lived in a heathen, pagan environment for 75 years; and out of that background he gained the lofty title of "Friend of God".

In our day we have access to a tremendous amount of Spiritual light, and so it would seem very possible to reach the high calling of "Friend of God". If you don't know Him, it's because you've chosen not to. You have chosen spiritual poverty. Abraham chose. He exercised his option for the highest and the best. Abraham was ready to believe and obey God. To believe without obeying is useless, but to obey without believing is impossible! Abraham believed God and obeyed God. In Abraham's case, life didn't begin at 40; it began at 75. It was then that God called him. It's never too late!

Abraham never wrote a book, gave a prophecy, or sang a song and yet Isaiah called him the Father of the Faithful and Friend of God! Abraham was not perfect: He waivered once in a while. You don't have to be perfect to be used of God, we are all flawed somewhere.

Abraham listened when God spoke. Learn to know the voice of God like Abraham, Samuel, and so many others. Does God speak audibly to us? Not very often. It's hard to describe how He speaks, but if you're open to His leading, He'll speak to your heart. You will know it is Him. Will you listen?

Are you sick of mediocrity, of casual commitment to God, of putting God and the things of God somewhere down near the bottom of your list? Wouldn't you rather be a champion for God? Everything else will fall into proper sequence.

The Deceptiveness of the Gradual

In the dictionary the word *deception* is defined as "fraud, double-dealing, trickery, the acts or practices of one who deliberately deceives, ingenious acts intended to dupe or cheat". *Gradual* is defined as follows: "moving, changing, or developing by fine, slight, and often imperceptible degrees, hardly noticeable".

In your drivers test manual there are a series of signs that are listed as signs that will save your life. One of these signs is "Yield". In traffic it's the smartest thing to do, but there are times in life when the yield sign can be fatal! Many times yielding is the first real step to the gradual drifting away. It starts with a compromise, and then, by imperceptible degrees, the person slips backwards.

In the church age and among groups and denominations, a falling away has come because, in the interest of unity, men began to compromise to "get along". Some have watered down the Pure Gospel to achieve that unity to try to please, at a great expense to the work of the Kingdom!

Let's get personal for a while today. Compromise will be fatal every time. The One we are following, who is the Fullness of the Godhead Bodily, cannot and will not compromise or be pleased with those who do. In Psalm 1, David is teaching three things in these Inspired Words: 1—We cannot accept the counsel of those outside of Christ, 2—We cannot be involved with those who live in open sin, 3—We must avoid the cynicism and unbelief of our society.

These Words are words of correction and warning. God inspired David to write them for our benefit. Satan is smart and he is deceptive. The pattern is specified. Please notice: walk, stand, or sit. First is casual contact—just walking and innocent fellowship, but this leads to standing, an agreement, a dialogue; and then sitting with them; this speaks of being involved.

In John 15:8 Jesus said, "If the world hates you, you know that it hated Me before it hated you!" I don't know what it will take for America to turn back to God. It started gradually, the Scopes Monkey trials of the 20s, the United Nations of the 40s, then the total kicking God out of public life in the 60s, and it's been downhill ever since. America needs to turn back to

God—true! But what will it take for individuals? What will it take to get you back on track again if you've drifted?

There's no place to compromise in Christianity. Jesus didn't. Paul didn't. Compromise opens the door to failure. Sure, it seems right. It seems like the thing to do. But the shores of time are full of wrecked ships that drifted with the tide into very rocky waters.

Getting Ready Today

In today's church world there's a message that is becoming almost obsolete. If it's not completely avoided, it's being watered down. It's the message of the Coming of the Lord, preceded by the Rapture of the Church. The confusion goes from Kingdom teaching where we, the Church, will clean up the world and get it ready for the Lord to come back. Then we have the a-millennial view that says there will be no rapture, no marriage supper, and no 1,000-year reign. There are those who do not believe that we are in the Last Days concerning God's Time Table. I don't know what you personally believe, or if you even think about it very often, but God has impressed on me to remind you what the Bible has to say and compare it to the events in today's world in light of clear Scripture.

We are living in the last days and our day of opportunity is here. Don't be lulled to sleep by easy living and the Laodicean syndrome of Revelation 3: neither hot nor cold, but lukewarm. They were lukewarm because they had lost their zeal, their love for souls, and their love for the Lord. Their vision of the Judgment Seat of Christ had faded. The II Peter 3:14 challenge to be diligent had fallen on deaf ears. The longsuffering of God is Salvation. His hand of mercy that withholds judgment is to give us an opportunity to persuade men and women to receive Christ to salvation. One of the signs that Jesus gave, one of many, was the sign of Noah. God warned them through that boat-building preacher for 120 years, but they didn't have time. They were eating and drinking, marrying and giving in marriage. It was business as usual until the flood came and God shut the door!

In Luke 17 Jesus also mentioned Lot, "But the same day that Lot went out of Sodom it rained fire and brimstone out of Heaven and destroyed them all!" It's a fact, what we know as the Church Age will not continue indefinitely. God has plans for a mass exodus of his people before the destruction comes. Noah got out before the flood. Lot got out before the fire. The fact of the removal of the church will be followed immediately by the fact of judgment! That's why we give altar calls, and that's why we weep over lost souls. That's why we invest thousands of dollars in missions. It's time to persuade men because we know the terror of the Lord.

Peter reminds us in verses 3 and 4 of Chapter 3 there are scoffers who ask the question, "Where is the promise of His coming?" The Bible is full of answers to that question. There are 39 Old Testament Books with different divisions: The Pentateuch, or the 5 books of Moses, 12 Historical books, Joshua to Esther, 6 books of Poetry, Job to Lamentations, and 16 major and Minor Prophets, Isaiah to Malachi. In each of these books you'll find the promise of His return. They all talk about it. In Genesis 3:15, "The serpent shall bruise His heel" (Calvary); "Jesus shall bruise his head" (His second coming when Satan will receive his final blow). Psalm 22 talks about His death; Psalm 23 about His presence with us now, and 24 is a prophetic psalm that will be fulfilled. In Isaiah 61: 1-2 the prophet specifies the exact ministry of Jesus, and Jesus confirms it in Luke 4: 18-19.

All over the four Gospels we read of His coming. Revelation is almost totally dedicated to the Promise of His Coming. So, scoffer, the answer to the question is in every book of God's Holy Word. I read the papers and see the promise of trouble in the Middle East and I say, "Jesus is Coming". The biggest battle is over God's promise to Abraham. Nations are in distress, swords are rattling, and sides are being taken. Iran,

Iraq, Syria, Lebanon, and then Libya and Egypt. Look at the map. In the center of all this you see Israel.

That's why we persuade men. It's high time to wake out of sleep and put God back on the throne of your life. Get your Spiritual direction off of the back burner and into the main stream of your living. Jesus is coming soon.

If you're not ready to meet Him, why not get ready today?

Moses Had 20/20 Foresight

It seems that we're all blessed with 20/20 hindsight. "If only I knew then what I know now!" How often have you said that? It's in Hebrews 11, the great Bible Hall of Faith, God's great cloud of witnesses who stand as role models of faith for all of us, that we learn so much about foresight. Faith is substance and evidence—evidence of things not seen! It's through faith that we understand the miracle of creation. The worlds were framed or created by the Word of God. God said! —and it was so. I wasn't there, so I understand it and believe it by faith. Those who deny it have never come up with a better explanation. The best they could concoct was a cosmic accident—a big boom—and here we are! We must have faith in order to please God for we must believe that He IS, and He rewards them that diligently seek Him. God said it and that settles it.

I would like to refer you today to one of these great heroes. He was the George Washington of his day. The Jews today still hold in great reverence Moses, their liberator. But Moses looked ahead—even past the Jews of today, with tremendous foresight and saw Him who is invisible. If the Jews only knew what

Moses knew through Faith they would also see their true liberator, Jesus the Messiah! Jesus—the One who will come after the great tribulation period, when Israel's back is against the wall. When they're surrounded on all sides, with no friend in sight, He will come in the clouds of Heaven and then they will see Him whom Moses saw by faith when he was still in Pharaoh's house.

He was called the son of Pharaoh's daughter by the Egyptians, but refused to accept that title. It is believed that Pharaoh was Rameses II. If you would go to Egypt today you could go to the Cairo Museum and see the remains of Rameses II. He's just a dried up shell of an ancient human being who lived thousands of years ago. I've heard it said that "memories are the companions of old age; choose them wisely". When a person is old he is the finished product of his yesterdays. His own decisions develop the pattern that his life will take. All that is left are memories of the past, and those memories will bless or condemn.

When you think of the great Pharaoh, Rameses II, and read Hebrews 11: 24 and 25, it comes home to you with the illumination of lightning. Moses' decision that he made through foresight takes on a whole new meaning. If Moses had not refused to be called the son of Pharaoh's daughter, if he would have compromised and refused to believe the promises of God, he could be to this generation today just another dried up mummy on display in a museum in Egypt.

The works of Moses and his teachings have inspired millions and influenced millions down through history. Wherever the Bible has been read, wherever the Word of God has been preached, the name of Moses is respected.

What made the difference? Why are all the works of Rameses dead while the works of Moses are eternal? The answer is simple, yet it's awesome! The difference was the choices that they made! Rameses chose Egypt: the world, its power, its wealth, its philosophy, the present luxuries.

Moses chose a different route, "rather to suffer affliction with the people of God ... esteeming the reproach of Christ greater than the riches and the treasures of Egypt!" for he had respect unto the recompense of reward! Moses had foresight. The Amplified Bible says that Moses was aroused by Faith.

He became excited. The choice he made was a result of total trust in the Word of God! Moses saw Him who was invisible, went on and chose those things that were incorruptible and through those choices was used of God to do the impossible. God only gives you Faith to do the impossible. The possible does not need Faith.

The decisions you make, the memories that come as a result of those decisions, will depend on your present priorities—the choices that you make right now will effect you for eternity.

Is It Hard to Be A Christian?

There are many misconceptions or wrong ideas about what it means to be a Christian. You hear statements like: "I would like to be a Christian, but I could never live the life." "I'm too weak." "It's hard to live for Jesus." "What's the use of trying, I'll just fall back again" and the reasons go on and on. For many people it's almost like having a toothache and yet being afraid to go to the dentist. The mental horror that we put ourselves through is unbearable: far worse than the treatment of the dentist. But when you get over the fear and you are walking around without the toothache, you're glad that you went. The idea that it's a chore or a burden to receive Christ and to make Him number one in your life is an idea that comes directly from the father of lies himself.

Let's look at several wrong ideas about Christianity.

First, there's the misunderstanding as to the part that feelings play in the plan. Sometimes we in the ministry overplay the feelings part, but the new birth does not depend on feelings! Feelings many times are a result, but repentance is an act of the will. I do what it is obvious that I must do. I turn around because I'm headed in the wrong direction. A person may calmly and collectively move toward Jesus just as they would make an important business decision. What happens outwardly varies, but it's what happens inwardly that counts. The Christian life is the right thing to do. Anything else is wrong.

Next, there's a misunderstanding as to the **conviction** of sin. Many have the idea that God has to scare you, and sometimes He does, but that's not the general rule. I've had my way long enough and the results are all in the loss column. Convincing comes before conviction. It's a sober moment. That moment can be resisted and it often is. If it's postponed or put off, then the pressure is on. There's struggle and unhappiness. It becomes a Spiritual battle. The Holy Spirit says NOW—Satan says NOT NOW. It's a situation that has to have an answer, or a choice.

There's also a misunderstanding as to the duties that a Christian life will involve. This is a real scare tactic of Satan's. Don't cross bridges till you get there. Once your soul's destiny is decided, then you'll presently know what to do with your life—and God's choice for you will be the best. You'll say, "I couldn't have planned it better."

Here's one that the devil will use to scare you out of becoming a Christian: The misunderstanding about giving up things. The Christian life is not planned to be miserable or uncomfortable. Satan whispers, "You'll never have another good time. It's sin to have fun." What cheap shot of Hell. Hogwash! I've had more fun living for Jesus than I've ever seen the world have. The Christian life is not an endless list of "thou shalt nots." It's like giving up prison for a life of freedom, or like giving a hospital stay for a Hawaiian vacation. What fun is there in the devil's crowd? You get wrong answers instead of right. You suffer guilt and a sprained conscience. It's more fun to help people than to hurt people. Salvation is so valuable that whatever it takes is a small price to pay. I confess that religion has made a relationship with Christ scary. Somber gray stone buildings, somber looking frowning clergymen, dismal music, long lists of don't—wrappings that fade and grow old quickly. That's what we've presented Christianity as to much of our world. There's life, and light, and joy, and happiness, and love, and fellowship, and exciting music, and a thrilling lifestyle. Jesus is a friend. He's sociable. He likes people. I like what I read about Jesus. He says, "Be of good cheer" (Matthew 14:27). Try it; you'll like it.

There's a lot of misunderstanding about the conditions of salvation. I don't even need to understand all about the Bible before I can become a Christian. You may not have another hour to get saved. We need to do first things first. I can't find forgiveness without God. I can't be clean without the Blood of Christ. Salvation is based on Faith in Jesus alone. Surrender your will to Him. To reject Jesus is eternally wrong. To receive Jesus is eternally right.

Whitewashed or Washed White

We're living in a day of cover-ups. If you're as old as I am, you remember whitewash. In the Tom Sawyer story we've all read where Tom was whitewashing a fence and through some deceptive maneuvering convinced several of his friends to finish the job for him. Whitewash was used often to freshen up fences or structures. It's a mixture of water and lime with some cohesive ingredient. To whitewash is to cover up. Webster says, "An act of glossing over or exonerating." If the rain came before it set, it would drop to the ground. When allowed to dry, it gave the building or fence a new look—a surface beauty that brightened the neighborhood. It was easily rubbed off and eventually fell to the ground in little pieces.

Our experience in Christ must be more than surface. We've got to be more than a landfill covered with snow. When the snow melts, the trash is soon exposed again. To be whitewashed is to admit that the gospel is true, to confess that God is good, and that He is worthy to be praised and to be served. You confess your allegiance to Him, but the depth of experience and change is not there. There's got to be a purging, a complete wash down. In the body shop business, they at times have to get down to the bare metal and start over.

In Psalms 51, David prayed for 2 things: Forgiveness and Cleansing. Would you argue with me that many times we stop too soon? We encourage people to seek forgiveness "Lord, forgive me. I'm sorry for my sin," but we stop there. What I want to tell you and remind myself today is that you can never be happy without cleansing. You can't be cleansed until you seek forgiveness, but you not only must be forgiven, but also washed white! David said, "Blot out my sins, and wash me and cleanse me!" The forgiveness is on the basis of God's mercy—giving me something that I don't deserve. He's not saying "take it easy on me God—it's my first offense—look at my good points and my good marks—I mean, it was a tough one—nobody could have made it". David called on God just like the lowest of the low. There was no self-righteousness. There were no excuses. He didn't blame his wife for his loneliness, or say, "I needed some attention." If you are hiding excuses, there will be no forgiveness. Jesus is looking for total surrender. It's wonderful to be forgiven—whether by a wife or husband or a friend or a creditor. It's sweet. But however sweet the sound, it doesn't remove the spot. David wanted a thorough job—bare metal, if you please! His prayer was "cleanse me—wash it out". Apply your Heavenly spot remover. Help me to be clean from wrong passion and fleshly appetites! That's what Paul meant when he prayed, "Sanctify me wholly" (Thessalonians 5:23). I'll not be satisfied till I know that I know that I know that I'm cleansed!

The bottom line: before God can do the complete job on you, you've got to come to Him, broken and willing. There His love can heal you. The king's horses and the king's men can't put Humpty together again. But the KING can do it!

To be clean and pure before God is the best way to live! It's the only way to live! Fall toward God. Fall into His arms just as you used to fall toward sin. He'll clean you up today!

Come Now – Let's Reason Together

Here is an invitation from the God of Creation to dialogue, "Let's reason together" (Isaiah 1:18). What an appealing invitation! The Bible calls for reason. I Peter 3:15, "Be ready always to give an answer to everyone that asks you—a reason for the hope that is in you!" In Romans 12 the apostle calls us to "reasonable service". Christianity is not a vague philosophy or the product of myth. It is not something concocted or conjured up by a witch doctor or a new age guru. It's not superstition or magic. It's not a "hope so" pie in the sky, by and by—not at all. Our faith is based on an invitation from the God of the universe to "reason together". There's never been a greater opportunity!

Do you know that the Gospel Message is for the whole man—and must be delivered that way? We have fallen into the trap too often of appealing only to the emotion. Thank God that emotion is involved, but it's more than the beat of the song or the supernatural manifestation. Too many stop there and miss the whole point. It's for the whole person, not just the part that can be so easily moved. I'm convinced that the preaching of the Gospel should not only appeal to our emotions, it must also challenge our intellect. We have a fantastic brain that needs to kick in to be engaged when the Word of God is opened. We are thinking creatures—and that sets us apart from the animals that only react to instinct. God has given us the gift of reason. What the Word of God declares is sensible and reasonable. I will not stake my eternal soul—my eternal destiny—on some new fad.

There's nothing bazaar or irrational about God's call. It makes sense. "Let's reason together," saith the Lord! When you understand the invitation you want to begin right now! When we get to this point, then our emotions get involved. My spirit is connecting with God's Spirit—and it effects my emotions. It creates a rejoicing. That's what caused the psalmist to shout aloud so often, "Bless the Lord, O My Soul, and all that is within me!"

The Gospel story, whether in the preached word, a song, or a testimony, appeals to my emotions. It surely does! There's joy and hope and freedom. It stirs me and makes me desire what God offers—and I respond with emotion! It is appealing to my mind, but it also must appeal to my will. God expects something from me. I can't remain neutral. The reasonable word makes it clear as a bell that I have to decide God's way and I must do something now! You can't straddle the fence. You can't play games about eternal life. How long can you realistically stay uncommitted to God?

A person doesn't come unless the Holy Spirit draws him. It's dangerous as well as eternally unreasonable to presume that He will always excuse your rejection and ignore His drawing.

God is calling us to come to Him! That's what separates the Gospel from the religions of the world. Religion tells the story of a man's search for God. Christianity is God's search for man. That's the tremendous difference.

There's no neutral ground offered. Receive and enjoy! Refuse and suffer!

It's a fantastic offer—and very real! He's waiting for your response!

Possessing Your Inheritance

It appears to me that in these days God is looking for a people who are willing to enter into a place of maturity in Him—a people who are fully possessing their rightful inheritance. He has given us the incentive, the tools, the power and the provision so that we don't have to fail! This is a specific invitation from Jesus. "Enter in"—an imperative—a command. You enter in! Not "I will if I feel like it", but an urgency. Be diligent. Luke's version says, "strive to enter in—many will seek to enter in and will not able!" The word "strive" requires effort and commitment on our part. The Greek word that KJV translated as *strive* is *agonizomai,* which is where we get the English word *agonize*: to contend for, to struggle. It's used to describe an athlete who is a winner. I Corinthians 9:25, "A man that striveth for the mastery is temperate in all things. Now they do it to obtain a perishable crown, but we (we strive—we agonize) to obtain an incorruptible crown."

Why do so many fall away or fail? The problem is not with the Lord. It is with us. Philippians 4:13, "I can do all things through Christ who empowers me from within." I Timothy 6:12, "Fight the Good fight of faith.

Lay hold on eternal life." Or better said, labor fervently to enter in!

Jesus talked about a strait gate. The Greek word is *stenos*. You've heard of a straight jacket. It's the same word—a strait gate, hard, difficult and full of pressures and hardships. It's not easy because it runs counter to natural instincts or at least natural desires. Simply said, it's the way of the Cross! There's no small print in the contract. Deny yourself or give up your right to life in a total commitment to Him!

The central message of the Word is the Lordship of Jesus Christ. Seek Him first. Let Him rule and reign in your lives. He wants to establish His government in us. Before He can work out of you He must be in you.

There's a strait gate and a wide gate. The wide gate is to flow with the crowd, to swim with the current, or to co-exist or survive. But we're not here just to survive. We're here to conquer, to win the race—to attack the gates of hell. The Word says that the gates of Hell will not prevail against us.

So many drop out—and for the silliest reasons. You've heard them and so have I. You may have given them. Let's grow up today. The secret to not dropping out is to be a striver. There's an Old Testament example in Exodus 10:26, "Our cattle also shall go with us—not a hoof shall be left behind—for we must take all to serve the Lord our God and we know not with what we must serve the Lord until we come hither."

The Hebrews were finally set free from the slavery of Egypt. When Israel marched to the Red Sea not a hoof was left behind. What is our lesson here? We need to strive to enter in at the strait gate—to make a clean break with the world. It's called total consecration! A hoof left in Egypt becomes Egypt's property. It becomes something that Pharaoh could tempt the people with to return to the old life!

How does that compute today? The hoof may represent something of the old life that a Christian tolerates in his heart. Something he just can't give up completely. It's part of the world, and if left unconquered it will sap your spiritual strength and rob you of your inheritance.

We need to succeed through His strength, not ours. Moses tried it in his own strength 40 years earlier and failed—until he relied on God and won! We have the same God on our side today.

It's Time To Change Sides

The old rocker Bob Dylan wrote, "Ya gotta serve somebody." And it's true! You belong to someone, and when your master is the devil it stinks! The worst possible result of a life of sin is happening—you belong, and when you belong to Satan it's hard to quit! It's a lot easier to start than to quit. It's worse than belonging to a crime syndicate or a drug cartel. You can't get loose. You may laugh and mock, but to be incorporated with Satan—to be mortgaged by the prince of darkness—is the ultimate bondage. You are not free to do as you please. Paul said it like this in Romans 7:19-20, "For the good that I would do, I do not; but the evil which I would not, that I do. Now if I do that I would not, it's no more I that do it, but sin that dwells in me" (and controls me). It's a terrifying experience. It caused Paul to cry out in agony, "O wretched man that I am! Who shall deliver me from this walking death?" (Romans 7:24) You can hear that cry at every bar room or crack house, every nightclub, and every house of perversion. It's never easy to serve the devil. Solomon knew. He said, "The soul of the unfaithful person feeds on violence" (Proverbs 13:2). Verse 15 says, "The way of the transgressor is hard!"

Who says so? God says so. God tells us that the sinner is tied to the devil. It's their bondage and their shame. You can call it mistakes, or blunders—convincing yourself, "it just happened," "I didn't mean to cheat," "I didn't intend to hurt anyone," but the fact is, it was a devilish thing. You sided with the bad.

To serve Satan is to walk hand and hand with rebellion. Satan takes everything that is good and makes it bad. You become his agent.

You can't hide behind "The devil made me do it". Look what it's done to your marriage, to your conversation, your speech, your thoughts, and your perverted imagination! You're not your own! Why does this happen? God says that it is "Because you are serving the wrong master".

Receive Jesus and you receive deliverance. Something goes out when He comes in. Ask the delivered addict. Ask John, the Apostle. He had a temper then Jesus filled him with His love! Jesus chased selfishness out of Zacchaeus and filled him with generosity.

Jesus won't force new life on you or into you, but He offers it to you as a choice. John 1:12 says, "As many as received Him". Choose Him! He has the authority. Only He can destroy the works of the devil. He's Heaven's demolition expert.

There it is. It's a single choice. Either serve Jesus or serve the devil. Your eternal destiny depends on it. Either Heaven or hell has begun for you already. I don't have to tell you. You already know. Choose life today.

Jesus and the Rich Young Man

Matthew 19: 16-22, "And, behold, one came and said unto him, 'Good Master, what good thing shall I do, that I may have eternal life?' And He said unto him, 'Why callest thou me good? There is none good but one, that is, God. But if thou wilt enter into life, keep the commandments.' He saith unto Him, 'Which?' Jesus said, 'Thou shalt do no murder,' 'Thou shalt not commit adultery,' 'Thou shalt not steal,' 'Thou shalt not bear false witness,' 'Honour thy father and thy mother,' and, 'Thou shalt love thy neighbor as thyself.' The young man saith unto him, 'All these things have I kept from my youth up. What lack I yet?' Jesus said unto him, 'If thou wilt be perfect, go and sell what thou hast and give to the poor, and thou shalt have treasure in heaven; and come and follow me.' But when the young man heard that saying, he went away sorrowful, for he had great possessions."

Talk about a man that had it all going his way. He was rich, he was young, he was a ruler—one of the "who's who" crowd. From all outward appearances he had it made!

The man was asking, "Lord, what must I do? I want my life to count for something. I'm aiming higher than what I have—I'm a businessman and I want the best return for my investment." Jesus was ready with the challenge and pleased with the answers: "I had kept all of the commandments, my integrity is impeccable!" But he fell backwards toward the temporary and he went away, as many do, sorrowful! He knew he asked too much. If he had disagreed, he would have gone away mocking. But Jesus was right. His own heart condemned him.

No one who wants his or her life to really count can gain eternal life in any way but Christ's way! You have to let the shore lines go; the ropes that keep you tied to the dock of this world must be cut. It cost something, but it's worth the cost!

Jesus Noticed

The word *comfort* is a big word in the Bible. In First Corinthians 1:3-4, Paul gives this greeting, "Blessed be God Even the Father of our Lord Jesus Christ, The Father of Mercies, and the God of all Comfort—who comforteth us in all our tribulation, that we may be able to comfort them which are in any trouble, by the comfort wherewith we ourselves are comforted of God!" It's like a circle, never ending, always producing comfort.

In Matthew 8 there's a beautiful look into the compassion of Jesus. It was the end of a very busy, tiring day and finally they had reached their destination, the home of Peter in Capernaum. We're not told what type of a home it was: probably humble and comfortable. Maybe a net hanging on the wall or some other tool of Peter's trade or a picture of a boat. They were looking forward to a well-deserved break, perhaps sitting down to the evening meal, when Jesus noticed (I love those words), "Jesus *noticed* Peter's mother-in-law was sick". **He noticed!** Not many do today. That's His greatness. He is Sensitive and Compassionate.

It wasn't easy to be a mother-in-law to Peter. Some of his old life resurfaced once in a while. Perhaps his marriage showed some stress and strain. Peter was loud and very unpredictable and sometimes insensitive. It's not nice to have company when you're sick. Peter didn't notice, but Jesus did. He noticed that she had a fever.

It's great to be a person that notices the needs of others. The more you wrap yourself in yourself the more misery you produce. Live for others, and you'll find the meaning of life. Acts 10:38 declares that "Jesus went about doing Good." There's always something to do and someone to help. Try to notice the flowers, the birds, and the children. Try to feel for others. It takes the boredom out of life.

Jesus noticed. It was part of His character. He noticed the lily, the sparrow, the fox, the farmer, the widow, and the bereaved, Martha in the kitchen, the soldier, Zacchaeus in the tree, and He noticed His mother "and comforteth her from the cross" (John 19:25).

What are you suffering from today? Perhaps you've suffered for a long time. The man who sold the liquor didn't notice. The pusher who sold the drugs didn't notice. The court that granted the divorce didn't notice the hurt. Even the church so often doesn't notice. You feel alone. You feel forgotten. You feel guilty, you feel afraid and suddenly Someone enters the room!

Give it to Jesus. He cares.

Majoring On Minors

We live in a society that has its priorities all messed up. Our Western culture places high value on putting a ball through a hoop—or hitting a ball 3 ½ times out of ten. Those who have mastered these skills make 10 times as much as the President of the United States. An average home in our area sells for $200,000 and 65,000 people will pay $80 per person to hear ear splitting sounds from a group of rock and rollers who look like they got their clothes at a Memorial Day yard sale in Dogpatch, and yet only 25 or 30 people will come out to hear a missionary talk about the harvest field of the world! It's a world of strange values.

When it comes to priorities we've got a short circuit somewhere.

In Genesis 1:16 we read some words that describe something totally indescribable with human language and understanding. "God made two great lights, the greater to rule the day and the lesser to rule the night. He made the stars also!" Moses wrote these words far before telescopes and Hubble space probes. How did he know that the sun was larger than the moon?

Ancient people believed that the moon was greater than the sun because it looked larger. They didn't know that it was much closer. Moses somehow knew the truth. He had Divine knowledge. The Bible is right all the time, and Moses writes in 5 words, "He made the stars also". In 5 words God dismissed the creation of all the stars in space.

Look at the contrast—there are over 50 chapters that discuss the construction of the tabernacle in the wilderness and its importance. That tabernacle has been gone for several thousand years. It was a temporary worship center—yet there are 50 chapters about the tabernacle and only 5 words about the stars.

In the book "Exploring Genesis", writer John Phillips wrote these words; "The Bible looks at things from quite a different perspective than we do. Why? The Bible is a handbook of Redemption. It was nothing for God to create—all He had to do was speak. But to redeem, He had to suffer, that's the perspective of the Bible!"

It's too easy for you and me to get a wrong perspective of what's real in life. The farther we get from the

Word of God, the farther we drift from His values. We get caught up in trivial pursuit and lose sight of eternal values.

On many issues we are way off base—forgetting issues that are truly important and wasting time and resources on what is insignificant.

Redemption was and is God's main issue. It's His mandate—win the lost at any cost.

The soul is the eternal part of man. Our bodies are temporary—they return to dust—yet our bodies receive the most attention and our souls receive the least attention. That's the opposite of God's perspective.

He went to great expense to redeem your soul. He's not concerned about the size of your home or your car, your financial holdings or your degrees. He is vitally concerned about your soul! Right now let the searchlight of Heaven expose your priorities. It is far better to be penniless than to lose your soul. Ask God to sharpen your perspective. Eternity depends on it.

My Forwarding Address

When I was in the real-estate world I would depend a lot on appraisers—people who are trained to evaluate properties. Their expertise was to place value on a piece of property. There are many ways that they use to come up with a fair value. In the same way, God sent Jesus to Earth to appraise your life and my life! His appraisal doesn't depend on bank accounts or net worth. Your possessions or lack of possessions mean nothing to Him. Your good health or lack of good health is irrelevant. In Luke 10:20 Jesus said, "The most important thing in all the universe is to have your name written in Heaven." To know that our name is written in Heaven is the greatest cause of rejoicing that we can have!

There are several things that are worth looking at concerning the conditions to meet in order to have our name written there. *1. I have no power to write it there myself.* It is impossible to write your name in Heaven! No king, or general, or president, preacher or priest, or singer, or hero could ever write his own name in Heaven. You may get onto our church roster, but that doesn't get it in the Lamb's Book of Life! You may be saying "My religion doesn't say it that way, or let me tell you about my religion." Save your breath. Religion isn't the answer. Ideas about religion don't count! The question is "Is your name written there?" Your opinion is ok, you have a right to it—but over there you'll need more than an opinion or theories. It's got to be God's terms! It's **His** Book and it's **His** way! *2. How can you be sure your name is there?* Hey, I don't want to guess—I can't afford to take a chance. I want to know—and it's possible to know or Jesus would not have told us to rejoice—you can't rejoice about something that you're not sure of. *3. John writes of the church at Sardis in Revelation 3. He tells us that Jesus examines church rolls.* He went over a long list of names—and made the statement in Revelation 3:4, "You have a few names among the many that I also have up here. They are folks who have not become defiled. Their walk matched their talk, they're in My Book!" What about the other names—they were on the church roll, but not in God's Book. There's a Heavenly Bookkeeper who keeps up-to-date books. Each name is written because it has a right to be there!

The requirements are clear and not negotiable. Ephesians 2:8, "For by Grace are you saved through faith, not of yourself, it's a gift of God."

He's knocking; why not let Him in?

Other Little Ships

In Mark 4:35–41 Jesus had just finished a busy day. He had preached and ministered to the crowd by the seaside and then had entered into a ship to continue the message. He taught them in parables (in this case the parable of the sower) and then He sent them home. He sent them away with their needs met and their hearts challenged. Now it was evening. I can almost hear Peter saying, "Lord, why don't we just check in at the local motel for the night and get up early to travel? I'm used to the sea, and nighttime isn't the best time to travel. We're tired and we need to rest". Why did Jesus propose to travel at night? I think it was so that He wouldn't lose any time being about His Father's business. He had to get to the other side because He knew there was work to do there. Nothing hindered Him from His mission.

The disciples immediately obeyed His commands. Verse 36 says they took Him as He was in the ship. No coat or cloak, and it was nighttime. They were facing a night of trouble. It was not uncommon, nor is it today, for storms to come up suddenly on that stretch of water. Those who follow Him must count on troubles

(Job 14:1). Sometimes He sends us into the teeth of the storm. But remember Hebrews 13:5, "I will never leave you," John 16:33. Jesus said, "In this world you will have tribulation, but I have overcome the world!"

Sure we'll see storms and trouble, but we're winners! Mark 4:36b states, "There were also with Him other little ships." Remember, we're never in the storm alone. The other little ships were experiencing the same fears and pressures as the disciples.

Here are several important points: 1. He stilled the storm *for all*. When you have victory in your life others are affected, and when you have defeat in your life others are affected. We're not in this alone. That's why those of us who profess Christ must weather the storms victoriously. 2. The influence of a life centered on Christ overflow to other little ships. There are little ships watching your life and being beaten by what they see. Be careful! 3. It pays to follow Jesus—the storms come, the winds blow, the rain falls, but it is great to know that the Master Pilot is in control when you hit the storm. Verses 37 and 38 say the waves beat into the ship. The adversary will try to put you under and try to fill your life up with problems that will choke out your victory and spiritual life. But thank

God He is in control! They learned that with Christ in the boat—though it may be tossed—cannot sink. Christ is always awake to the prayers of His people.

They needed not fear, but yet in our humanity we do sometimes doubt. Notice how quickly Jesus met the need. He has dominion over the winds, waves, storms, your habit, your sickness, your financial needs, and your spiritual needs. He has it all. Stop trying to row your own boat. Ask Him to take control. Jesus did it with just a word, "Peace Be Still". Only the Prince of Peace can bring peace.

How to Get Out of the Pressure Cooker

There's a verse that says, "Into every life some rain must fall"—that's true. Those who reject struggle miss growth. There are many Christians who ask themselves the question, "Why does it have to happen to me?" Sometimes we even allow ourselves to think that no one else is having any troubles. I've learned that behind every powerful life, every radiant person, there have been bitter testings. A life that is used of God generally has had some tremendous conflicts of Satan.

Paul had a personal problem. Even though he was a powerful giant killer for the Lord, as well as a man of experience, understanding, and knowledge, we learn from his own testimony that his personal struggle was not easy to handle. Paul opened his heart to God and to all of us. We have the advantage of his experience to learn some lessons for our own benefit. As Paul writes these words you sense three things: Frustration, revelation, and transformation. It was frustrating to this apostle to say, "There was given to me a thorn in the flesh, a messenger of Satan to buffet me" (2 Corinthians 12:7). Talk about human experience! We all can sympathize with Paul. Why would God choose a man like Paul to live with the pressure of a "thorn in the flesh?" We're not told what the thorn was, but whatever it was, we know it was hard. It may have been a personality weakness, a physical disability, or maybe even something in his Spiritual discipline. He could have faced a battle at every turn in the road or every step he took. Whatever it was, Paul was conscious of it and perhaps sensitive about it. Paul wanted to be set free from the "messenger of Satan that buffeted him". If only I could get this thorn out, I would be so much better if I could overcome this opposition. It was pressure. Why must I live under pressure? We have it today. If only I had a different job! If only this pain would go away. If only I had different in-laws…and on and on. We knock ourselves out. We pray. We groan. We wish and worry—just like Paul. It's persistent. It doesn't let up, and because of it there is disappointment—but the disappointment becomes a source of discipline. "For this thing I besought the Lord three times, that I may be rid of it" (2 Corinthians 12:8). Paul prayed about it. That's a great way to start. Too many times we wait too long to pray about it. "I besought the Lord." That's a strong word. It borders on begging. Definitely carrying a heavy burden. Paul felt it and it had to go!

Can you believe that if God is letting the pressure on that He'll also have provision for your need? He'll transform your weakness to strength. Don't you want to see His strength alive in you? Don't you want to see Him work? If you do, then let God make you what you ought to be—not what you'd like to be. God is looking for channels. If you long for victory over pressure let God transform your life!

How to Pray Effectively

Prayer is our most valuable source of spiritual power. The Bible records over 650 definite, specific prayers with no less than 450 recorded answers to prayer. Both in the Old Testament and New Testament men of God prayed. When there was no place to look they looked up and their prayers were heard.

Their prayers were more than recital of well-known phrases and well-worn ritual—they were outpourings of the heart. When they were surrounded by perils, persecution, pain and privations, they naturally turned to God believing that He was able to deliver them. They may have known little of the philosophy of prayer, and perhaps their posture was not right, maybe their techniques were crude, but they certainly knew the Power of Prayer! Here's a simple definition: Prayer is the desire, privilege, and opportunity of talking to God! It is a correspondence fixed with Heaven. Family prayer began when the first family was formed. Beginning in Genesis with Adam and Enoch and through to Revelation with John, man had communication with God. The New Testament is full of directions to pray for and seek after Spiritual blessings. He who is in good standing with God and works at prayer will see much accomplished. This applies to the individual and the nation.

There are several important principles that we must follow in order for us to be successful in our prayer life. Many Christians experience unanswered prayer because little things keep them from God. When we pray we must have His Mind (Philippians 2:5), we must correspond with His Will (Romans 12: 1-2), and we must be in harmony with His Wishes (Luke 11:3). God's conditions are clearly defined in His Word: humility, repentance, obedience, forgiveness, and faith are just a few. Our heart condition when we pray is very critical to our success in prayer.

I Timothy 2:5 states, "There is one mediator between God and Man: The Man Christ Jesus". Jesus loved to pray. As you study His life you find a beautiful pattern of a successful prayer life. Jesus taught the necessity of prayer by personal example. Prayer was a regular habit of Christ.

In His Name we have the greatest resource of Power at our disposal. He's waiting to hear from you.

Measured by the Plumb Line

About 6 miles south of Bethlehem is the village of Tekoa. Tekoa was a place where not too much of anything happened. It was just a crossroad town. Today it's about 5 acres of ruined village called Khirbet Taqua. There was a small-time shepherd in Tekoa named Amos. The word Amos means "burden bearer or one with a burden". This man lived up to his name. He didn't seem to have any rank or influence. He was not a professional preacher or prophet. He hadn't even gone to the school of the prophets. He wasn't a college graduate, but he knew God and God talked to Him! His flock of sheep was small and the desert lifestyle that Amos lived gave him much opportunity to think and to pray—and because of the time spent alone with God he had a communication that gave him clear judgment. The art of hearing from God and being heard of God is not developed in large crowds.

There's a qualification that God looks for that we miss too often. The combination of superior education and the anointing of the Spirit is hard to beat, but if I have to choose between "enticing words of man's wisdom", or the "demonstration of the Spirit and of Power", I'll choose the Spirit, for as Zechariah 4:6 tells us "it's not by might, nor by power, but by my Spirit". God asked for this poor man's personal opinion. Twice the Lord spoke to him and asked, "Amos, what do you see?" God cares what the common man thinks.

God sees and deals in potential and availability over ability all the time. God listens to those whom the world calls foolish. They have good eyes, a good mind and a good sense of values. God wants to know how things look to the average man. Amos represented the worker—the guy doing the average job, living in a small community. Amos didn't have any connections. He didn't belong to a special club, but God asked him for an opinion. Amos "what do you see" and I said "a plumb line".

In Webster's Dictionary there are several definitions of a plumb line, and they all have to do with vertical direction. "A lead weighted line to indicate vertical direction." A plumb line is the common tool of a mason or a carpenter. To Amos it was a symbol of testing. He knew that his generation had to be tested and plumbed. It had to be subject to Divine measurement. Every generation is subject to this plumb line. We need to use it to measure our culture, our marriage, our free time, and our entertainment. God is very concerned about our vertical relationship. As a believer I have the responsibility of using God's plumb line against our television, industry, against our education and institutions, against our government, and yes, even against the church!

Amos taught that against the brightness of God's Grace, sin is black. Sin is sin! He taught that mere ritual did not please God. Israel thought that God was some vain Monarch who was pleased with service and tradition. Amos also taught that God's dealing with men is for their discipline, not their doom. He did not forget God's Grace! He preached and taught restoration! Thank God that He's in the restoration business. He's the healer of broken hearts and lives!

In chapter 8:1 and 2, God has another object lesson for Amos. The question is the same: "Amos, what do you see?" "A basket of summer fruit." In the Hebrew the same word is used for "summer fruit" that is used for "end". Amos saw the end. His nation was rotten with corruption. We hope for the best, we hope for improvements, but the facts are facts, and facts are sometimes unpleasant. God is asking us today to take inventory. What do you see? God is not ignorant of our Supreme Court decisions. He overhears the counsels of our educators. He wants to make sure that we are seeing things as He sees them.

God allowed Amos to show Israel a happy ending. Verse 9:14, "and I will restore my people. I will set them free from the captivity and the rut that they're in. If they turn to me, I'll forgive and forget."

When Satan Knocks Let Jesus Answer

John 14 has been a source of comfort to countless people for centuries. It's often used to comfort the bereaved at a funeral. "Let not your heart be troubled" John writes that phrase twice for emphasis. Today I want to encourage you in the Lord. These are days when peace is a scarce commodity.

Have you ever been included in a will? Or have you wondered or wished that some wealthy relative had included you? People make wills every day. You must if your wishes are to be honored after you die. Many times friends as well as family are included in these documents.

There are many who are unaware of the good fortune of being included in a will. That seems impossible, but it's a fact. You may not realize this, but Jesus made a will shortly before He died on the cross. His generosity, which included you, is found in John 1 14:27, "My peace I leave with you, not as the world gives—but *my* Peace—so let not your heart be troubled and don't be afraid."

There's not a lot of peace in this world today. Tension and hostility are everywhere. Peace talks are tentative and very fragile; most of the time they don't work out. Whether it's an international situation or a personal relationship, real peace is hard to come by. Jesus made a great distinction between the peace that the world offers and His peace. He said there's a difference between His peace and the world's peace. In Isaiah 9:6 the prophet calls the future Messiah the "Prince of Peace". In Ephesians 2:13-14 Paul says that Jesus Christ is our peace. There is truly a difference. The peace that Jesus gives is not conditional or based on circumstances. It comes when you accept Jesus as your personal Lord and Savior. He then becomes our peace because He is perfect—our perfect peace is perfect.

The Peace of Christ does not depend on externals. It is permanent—in spite of adversity. In days of old, people who lived in fortified castles would dig deep wells inside of the walls to provide water when they were under attack. If they depended on outside sources they would be at the mercy of the enemy who could cut off their water supply. It works the same way when we have the Prince of Peace living inside of us. He is an inner source of peace and confidence. We are not victims of circumstances. Our peace is secure in His presence.

Don't wait until you can be the person God wants you to be. You can't! You come as you are and He makes you to be what you ought to be! Every time you try to do what's right without God's help, it causes more frustration.

Would you like perfect peace instead of guilt? Would you like perfect peace instead of frustration or anxiety? Ask Jesus to forgive you and take control of your life. When you've done it, start reading your Bible every day. Spend time in prayer. Join fellow believers in a local church. This will strengthen your new life—this peace lasts through eternity.

Is God Good?

"Orientation, disorientation and re-orientation." In Psalm 73: 1 the psalmist is giving the orientation (the mindset) that we have been taught that God is Good! "Truly God is Good to Israel". From childhood we've been taught that God is Good. We give our children little papers and mottos that say, "God is Good". We teach them little prayers "God is Great, God is Good, now we thank Thee for this food". We believe it as a child. We are oriented to accept that blindly—but life is real. Our orientation can soon be disoriented. If God is good, then why did this happen? Why did this calamity come? Why did God allow a terrorist attack on America? Verse 1 says, "God is Good". Verse 2 says, "but"—my mind set, my teaching, my faith as a child, is now being tested. My feet were knocked out from under me. I am wallowing in discouragement. I am disoriented. It's not like I thought it would be. I was blind-sided.

Preachers are prone to orient you to the fact that "God is Good". We sing worship songs: "God is so Good", "He is Lord", "Great Is Thy Faithfulness", and then someone will sing a special song that depicts a trial that they're going through or that they've gone through. "When shadows deepen and my heart bleeds"—and we see a contrast. Is God Good? Can I tell the 12-year-old whose father was killed at the World Trade Center that God is Good? Heavenly Father, you've taught us—our Fathers have taught us that You are Good—but it doesn't fit my life—it's not real!

There's healing virtue in taking God as a partner in your struggles. To open up to God and admit, "I know you're Good, but I nearly slipped".

Disorientation is tough. We've all been to the place of disorientation but ahead is re-orientation—and what a place to come to! David said, "It was too painful for me until I went into the Sanctuary of God—until I entered His presence." God can take the disorientation, when everything is ripped apart, and take Lordship over the situation and do His work beyond our comprehension in this terrible time in America. I had to get alone with God because I felt ripped apart. I could do nothing but get alone with God.

How did the psalmist get re-oriented? Just as you and I must; get alone with God and be open and honest with Him.

Disorientation comes and testing comes. It's a cycle that continues—and you can know beyond a shadow of a doubt that God is Good. It means more to you now that God has re-oriented you. Whenever my feet falter and I get ashamed before God I reach for His Hand my understanding grows. Verse 28 says, "It is good for me to draw near to God! He is a very present help in trouble!"

Is Your Joy Real or Imitation?

They say that imitation is the most sincere form of flattery. McDonald's is the perfect example. Soon after the Quarter Pounder was introduced, everyone in the business began to sell Quarter Pounder burgers. The McMuffin craze took off as well. Polaroid invented a camera with the ad line "It hands you the picture". The next year everyone's cameras were "handing out the pictures". It's called in sociology "the bandwagon effect". Americans have learned that it's easier to jump on someone else's wagon than to create their own tune!

Satan is an expert at trying to imitate the Joy of the Lord—or the shear ecstasy of the Christian Life. There are many "new and improved" versions of what Jesus taught.

Psychics, new age gurus, satanists and witches attract people who are interested in the supernatural. People offer their friends drugs to give them an easy "high". It's important for us to know what real joy or ecstasy is and what it isn't!

How can you tell the difference between the real and the false? It's not easy when the imitation and the imitators seem so appealing. I'm sure that you've heard of "fools gold". Iron Pyrite. The prospectors in the old west would carry a vial of acid, which would dissolve fools gold but would not affect real gold. When he was in doubt he would use a few drops of acid—it's called the acid test. You and I can use God's Word the same way. When "you're made an offer" or confronted by a lifestyle or a philosophy that promises a new high, give it the acid test from Scripture. Read Psalm 119:165, "Great peace have they who love your Word and abide by your standards". Give it the acid test of real peace. Those who live outside of God's joy, those who follow man's ways, (Isaiah 59:8) "the way of peace they know not! They have made them crooked paths and whosoever goes in them shall not know peace". Ecstasy means peace. A true experience with Christ will make a troubled person untroubled! If your pursuit of joy or happiness or thrills fill you with tension and fear or anxiety or stress it's imitation—not real—not satisfying.

The Peace of God, the Joy of the Lord, and Spiritual ecstasy renews you. It doesn't use you up; it fills you up. 2 Corinthians 4:16 "Therefore we do not lose heart...our inward man is renewed day by day!" A daily diet of the Word of God and fellowship with God through prayer will renew you. The peddlers of false joy or false ecstasy sell you a little routine or exercise, which will "expand your consciousness or lift you to a higher plane". The bottom line is boredom, emptiness and frustration!

The only real joy is in Christ. If it's anything else—if it doesn't glorify Christ—it will not bring peace to the inner person. They may sound alike and look alike, but the imitation will eventually be exposed! Colossians 3:23-24 states, "Whatever you do, do it heartily as to the Lord and not to men, knowing that from the Lord you will receive the reward of the inheritance, for you serve the Lord Christ". If you can't do it "heartily, as unto the Lord," it will not satisfy!

It's Good for What Ails You

During the early days of our country when the West was very young, medicine men would travel through the frontier peddling their wares: a bottle of colored water that was a cure-all no matter what the physical problem. This stuff could cure it quickly. The sales pitch was simple—it's good for what ails you!

I have a greater—a far greater cure-all to offer you today. In fact, we have the cure-all to offer the world today. It's an ointment, a salve, that when applied according to directions, takes care of whatever ails you! This cure heals the sorrows and sicknesses of mankind! In Luke 13:32 Jesus responded to the threats from Herod—the meanest man of his day—one who was totally ruthless when it came to the value of life, a wicked tyrant. They said "Jesus, run for your life! Herod has put out a contract on you!" Jesus sent a message back to Herod; "Go tell that fox" (sly, crafty, sulking, and cowardly fox*) amplified* "I do cures!"

The Name of Jesus and the Power of that name is a medicine for every sickness, both physical and spiritual. His Name is an ointment poured forth because it supplies healing and forgiveness.

I'm weary of seeing the terrible wounds that are a result of sin! Sin tears lives into shreds. Those who have become its victim suffer severe lacerations! You don't have to be a preacher to see the results of sin. It's devastating. The victim will tell you that "nothing is strong enough to break the chains of sin that bind me. I'm sick in my soul. I'm weary and defeated, frustrated and discouraged. I want to take my life. Who can help me?" I love what Jesus often said, "Wilt thou be made whole?" Do you want something that is guaranteed for what ails you? Sin tears people apart. Sin shatters dreams, and goals and high hopes. The result of moral disobedience is often physical sickness. Hatred destroys a marriage; families separate. It's so familiar today. Here's a caution: don't let sin get a foothold. Avoid compromising situations. Don't be flirtatious or careless in your interactions. It's dangerous and it's destructive. An aching conscience is unbearable. Guilt is a heavy burden to bear. But there's an answer: "What can wash away my sin? Nothing but the blood of Jesus!" How far will His love reach? When we say "Calvary covers it all" do we really understand the magnitude of that statement? There are no known limits to the Power of the Blood!

The Name of Jesus is our only hope in this life and the next. His Name brings comfort. His Name brings Mercy. What other name gives us this kind of hope? Trust Him. Confide in Him. His Name is a cure-all for what ails you today.

Jogging or Racing

It used to be when you would see a man running he was in a hurry to be somewhere. It was the normal thing to stop your car and give him a ride. Most of the time he would be glad to accept. Try that today. Pull alongside a runner and ask him if he needs a ride. He'll smile through his pain, wave and say, "No thanks, I'm not going anywhere". If you are not familiar with the current fad of jogging you could be a bit confused.

If he's not going anywhere, why is he running? He looks like he's about to fall over, he's in pain, he's sweating, and yet he's not going anywhere! Of course, we're wise to the ways of joggers. Some of us may even be joggers. They run several miles a day and end up in the same place where they started. Some run by the clock, one half-hour and stop, others by the lap. It's good. I'm becoming aware of the fact that the world is doing the same thing in practically every sense. There's a lot of action, a lot of activity, movement and momentum, but no achievement—not going anywhere. They argue yet they ignore the truth, they fight for peace but have no real peace or any concept of what peace really is. There's no peace without the Prince of Peace. They are studying, but the interest, the motivation, is for degrees rather than knowledge. "Ever learning but never coming to the knowledge of the truth!" 2 Timothy 3:7. They protest progress but have no better plan to offer. They want more money but don't know how to handle what they have.

The saddest thing is the fact that not only is the world jogging and going nowhere, but the church is jogging too. The church in general has lost its vision. here are a few that are going somewhere with vision and purpose—with a goal to establish a momentum toward God that will blow the gates of Hell of their hinges. I want to be a part of a church that torments Satan, but to many people church is just another jogging exercise. The same Sunday morning rip to the house of God once a week satisfies many church members. They live, work, play and worship without any long range plans. Never challenged to set goals or to go somewhere. That kind of a lifestyle leads to stagnation, which is living death! The Word says, "Where there is no vision the people perish," Proverbs 29:18. Jogging is good physical exercise, but spiritual jogging with no goal in mind is sure failure. We need to be honest. Whatever comes first in our lives is our goal. According to your first priorities, where are you heading? Righteousness (to be right with God) is a product of Faith. Let His approval be your goal, and you will find righteousness, peace, and joy in the Holy Spirit while you are still living on planet earth. One day we'll be with Him eternally, not by jogging but by going somewhere.

Grinding at the Mill

We live in an assembly age: an age of routine and sameness. The days between paychecks run together. We are in the world and daily we rub shoulders with unbelievers. The majority of Christians are sandwiched between non-Christians at the job. The same factory smells, the same idle talk, the same vulgar language, the same weekend stories, the same scenery, the same work. Thousands of believers are committed to unglamorous jobs, routine work, quotas, and the noise of clattering machinery that dulls the senses. They must serve Jesus in the midst of circumstances and an environment that is far from spiritual. Jesus called it "grinding at the mill": A very fitting description. But Jesus also promises a day when that boresome assembly line is going to get the shock of their life. A shocking surprise will bring the grinding to a halt for that day! These believers are what the church is made of, unsung heroes bearing under the burden and keeping the lamp burning in their soul even though it becomes a chore at times. There's a great lesson to be learned from the "Grinders at the Mill".

Jesus is showing us here, firstly, the importance of the soul! What makes one different than the other is they both have on the uniform of the job. The grind of life is evident in both. They are interlocked in the grind, and it's tiring. They feel hemmed in, like they're in a package. But the difference is on the inside. Inside the one: a new life. They are citizens of two worlds. Ezekiel spoke of the soul in 18:4, "The soul that sinneth it shall die". That's true. And the soul that believeth shall live! John 5:24, "Truly, truly, he that heareth My word and believeth on Him that sent Me shall have everlasting life!"

Socialism and communism, "the failures of the century", tried to chain the souls of men—to make them possessions of the state. Humanism does not know the value of the soul or how important the soul is to God. The soul of all improvement is the improvement of the soul. It's what's inside of me that counts. Two working side by side. One looking down and the other looking up! One is going to exit and the other will still be breathing dust and fumes under the reign of the anti-christ. Believe it or not, it's here in the Bible. Is it well with your soul?

I want to encourage you today. If your work seems small or trivial, and you wish there was some way to brighten up your corner, there is. Be renewed in the inner man. This may be the day of excitement on the assembly line. "One shall be taken"—it's you! That inner strength, and that hope, that comfort can be contagious to others!

The soul makes life beautiful—and Christ makes the soul beautiful! The difference between the two is this; one is focused on the coming of the Son of man, the other has no deliverer. One does not see what the other sees. There's no relief, and no promise of anything better—and the grind only makes them harder. The others see beyond the grind because of a relationship: a saving relationship. The believer is not part of the scene; we're just passing through.

Man divides people into many different classes by location, clothes, education, and job description—but not God! God looks at the heart. He doesn't see social status or denomination. To God, there are only two classes, lost or found—which boils down to taken or left. Nothing else that you have or desire can lift you of the grind. Only Jesus can do it.

Happiness Is the Lord

We are living in a day when discontentment is normal. There are discontented preachers, discontented church members, and discontented citizens of all races and stations of life. To be dissatisfied is not wrong. Dissatisfaction in some areas is good, for it breeds progress and makes things better. Discontent in that sense brings improvement, but the uneasy restless state of mind is not progressive or healthy. It brings misery to the person. Discontent dishonors God in that it says, "I don't like what God has chosen me to be."

I should never be content or happy headed in the wrong direction. I have to be restless when I look at what the world system displays. It's not wrong to want to go higher to advance and get ahead. I am ever learning and increasing in knowledge, so in that sense I am not content, I'm working toward a better me. But even contentment must have a balance—must be careful of priorities.

People think that if they could change marriage it would be Heaven; then they go and find an equal, if not worse, state of affairs. We get married at the altar, and if we keep the altar in our marriage it will last. Students think that if they change courses at school they would magically get ahead. Workers want their income to be greater than their input. That's why we have strikes. You know and I know that everybody loses when there is a strike. Church bouncers are looking for the perfect fellowship and a perfect Pastor that preaches messages that don't step on toes. When they think they find one, they join and ruin it. The middle-aged person wants to look younger. They try facelifts and plastic surgery, and try to forget birthdays. The rich want to give their riches away to please conscience and the poor are trying to get it. The lady with a closet full has nothing to wear! No one knows what level of living will make them comfortable. The thin want to gain weight, and the pudgy want to lose weight. The weather is never just right. The farmer or the businessman always wants more profit. Some men are still looking for the perfect woman, and women are looking for the perfect man. Our society is worried most of the time. Property owners wish they were renting, and apartment dwellers can't wait to own their own home. Investors have fears of losses. The socialite is sick and tired of parties and small talk.

Humanity is disturbed and hurting. When you strip off the surface you find that fear is gnawing in the inner life. Is it possible to be at peace with God on the inside? Is it all in the by and by, or can I have abundant life here and now? Granted, there are people that make a career and a lifestyle out of being discontented. They don't want to be happy and are mad at you if you are. I feel sorry for people like that. Paul said it well—those who have no hope are miserable.

Too many are living by an entirely wrong rule: man's happiness is in things. That abundance is in the amount of things we possess. That peace of mind is dependent on outward circumstances rather than the condition of the soul and spirit. Peace of mind is dependent on inner qualities! *Having* can never satisfy, *being* is rewarding. It is what I *am,* not what I *have* that makes the difference! I am happiest when God has His way.

Circumstances are not my master. It's not *where* I am; it's *what* I am. Paul learned to be bigger than his circumstances. He found happiness in a personal, loving relationship—not a religion - but a relationship with Christ. If it pleased Jesus, it pleased Paul. Where can I find contentment? Only in the Lord.

A Fatal Oversight

The Book of Deuteronomy is the last book of the Pentateuch—or the five books of Moses. The name comes from two Greek words *deuteros* meaning second, and *nomos* meaning law. It is basically a repetition of the law given prior to Israel entering Canaan. The previous generation had died in the wilderness and so the new generation needed to know what the Lord had said. The setting is on the plains of Moab. Moses is the speaker. It's his last charge to the people. After this final instruction, the Word tells us that Moses died. He was 120 years of age, and his "eyes were not dim nor his natural force abated" (Deuteronomy 34:7). He said what God wanted said and he said it the way God wanted him to say it. The Word says, "There was not a prophet like Moses whom the Lord knew face to face!" (Deuteronomy 34:10)

The main theme of Deuteronomy is the word *remember*. Don't forget. Don't forget the Law: the covenant: the past bondage: the Great deliverance: Divine presence and leadership: your past sins: Divine judgment: and the old landmarks! Don't forget. It's so easy to forget. How often have I forgotten something:

very often something important. Every parent has heard their child say, "I forgot the dishes, my homework, to take out the trash, to cut the grass." I forgot. They never forget the TV show, or the day that allowances are due. In the natural process of growing up we expect it; although some are more scatterbrained than others. But in the Spiritual sense as well and in the natural, forgetfulness can be fatal!

What is it about us that causes us to forget so quickly? We forget friends, relationships, we forget decency, and tragically we forget eternal values! Our nation has thrown away the things that made us strong. What made America strong is our commitment to God. We were founded on God and we will only stand as we remain founded on God!

Our history books remind us over and over again how we turned to God in times of trouble. It's as old as the Bible—the victory cry from every godly nation is "the Battle is the Lord's".

But times have changed. We're becoming eroded from the inside: nationally and spiritually. Marriage vows can be "take it or leave it". The Lord's day is a time for fun and games—racing, fishing, camping, hiking, visiting, etc.—anything but church! Not only the Lord's day, but the Lord's name as well—cursing His holy name, spitting on Biblical morality, addiction, cheating, lying, coveting, sexual liberty. Situational ethics direct our lives. No matter who says what, pre-marital or extra-marital sex is sin. It's listed in the Word along with murder. God does not turn his head from rebellion against His morality. Girls, have the guts to say "no" and if you lose the guy, you didn't have much anyhow! Trust God to find you a real man who respects you for who you are, not for what you do for him! The free-thinking society that has forgotten God leads to death! You may snicker. I hope you're not, but just look at history; sixteen major civilizations have fallen because of the violation of God's laws! Proverbs 14:34, "Righteousness exalts, but sin is a reproach." "The wages of sin is death."

Lukewarmness leads to coldness, and you reason "God is a God of love". He'll understand. I'm only doing what I have to do to make it. But you've forgotten something: God's laws, God's holiness, and God's direction in your life. You've forgotten that there is a heaven and there is a hell! Eternity is very sure!

When you stand before God you can't say, "I forgot", "I meant to live for Christ", "I meant to receive Him", "I meant to call the Pastor", "I knew that I should, but I forgot". "I mean, they were really important to me God". "Really, I was going to get around to you eventually, but I forgot".

Careless neglect—ignoring God's direction—is fatal. I pray that the Holy Spirit will reach you right now and remind you that now is the accepted time. Today is the day of salvation!

What's So Amazing About Grace?

The gospel of self-help is a popular gospel today, but it's not working. The only thing that it's producing is a lot of financial success to those who sell it. The problem is that we're told that by our human will we can improve ourselves. May I remind you that if I can save myself I wouldn't need Jesus! He died in vain if I could please God on my own. The fact is that a loving and Holy God chose to send His Son to suffer for sin rather than inflict suffering on us. Why He did it and how He did it are what is so amazing about it. It really is Amazing Grace! This is the faith part of the equation. It was all done before you and I were born. God accomplished it without the help of a committee or a denomination. It was His sovereign Will and His action on our behalf that produced Ephesians 2:8-9. You and I are saved by what God has done for us! Grace covers all that Christ did for us at the cross and still does for us through the Holy Spirit! It is God's heart toward me. I did not deserve his response. Romans 5:8, "But God commanded…while we were yet sinners Christ died for us!" God is outgoing toward us. It's described well in the story of the prodigal, Luke 15:20, "While he was yet afar off his father saw him, and was moved with compassion and ran, fell on his neck and kissed him!"—pig pen smell and all. That's the God of the Bible. He is merciful and full of grace and truth!

Jesus was full of Grace—gracious to women, children, the sick, the poor, the crippled, the widows, and the rich. His purpose was to destroy the works of the devil by showing us what God is like. Jesus loved mankind and got close to mankind. That's the way God is, and He proved it on the cross. How much does God love me? Romans 8:32, "He that spared not His own Son, but delivered Him up for us all now shall He not with Him also freely give us all things?" So where do I fit into this picture? My only responsibility is to receive. It's a gift of God! I don't have a right to it, but I'm faced with it. No matter what, I can't avoid it; it's confrontational. Calvary is too big to be avoided. If I receive, it is my salvation. If I reject, it becomes my condemnation. It's an offer I'm foolish to refuse.

John 1:12 states, "As many as received Him" God can handle any run on the bank of Heaven. He yearns for us to tap our assets. It's waiting for us to enjoy it. The picture is complete. Whether you accept or reject doesn't change God's plan, but I'll tell you this from personal testimony as well as Paul—you can never be satisfied until you are satisfied in Jesus.

People are confused by religious phrases and terms. "There is a fountain filled with Blood" scares people, but let me remind you what that conveys: Christ alone made available forgiveness, cleansing, and restoration for all men. Nothing equal or better has ever been produced. It's real and it works.

Salvation

The Fundamental Doctrine of the Bible is Salvation. In Protestant Christianity there are numerous denominations and equally as many definitions and interpretations of Scripture.

In Evangelical groups and fundamental Christianity, among all of our differences we believe in one basic doctrine; John 3:3, "Ye must be born again".

Jesus called it being born again, Paul defined it as being saved (Acts 16:31). You may call it regeneration, redemption or whatever else fits. I think the word salvation describes the experience well. Salvation is God loving His creation so much that in spite of man's fall God provided Himself a supreme sacrifice for sin in the person of His Son, Jesus Christ.

Jesus. The name Mary had no other choice but to give her Son. "He shall save His people from their sins!" (Matthew 1:21) Jesus means one "who brings salvation". Jesus never strayed from His calling. The most read and loved verse in the Word is John 3:16, and from it we understand the reason for His coming.

"For God so loved that he gave". Luke 19:10 also describes why He came. "He came to seek and to save the lost". I Timothy 1: 15 says, "He came to save sinners". Salvation began in the Garden of Eden. It wasn't a last-minute plan of God. God's pattern was set. As a covering for sin, blood was shed. God provided animal skins as a covering. Hebrews 9:22 states, "Without shedding of blood there is not remission for sins". The first formal sacrifice was found in Genesis Chapter 4 where Able provided a pleasing sacrifice and Cain went his own way.

Israel in Egypt. Once again a blood sacrifice—a first born male lamb without spot or blemish. The blood applied was the sign of obedience to God. "When I see the blood I will pass over you" (Exodus 12:13). Then Jesus came. He became the Supreme Sacrifice. Jesus came for the single purpose to reconcile man unto God (II Corinthians 5:18). Because God's requirement was shed blood it meant that Jesus had to die. Through His death, man again has direct access unto God. "Now there is one Mediator between God and man and His name is Christ Jesus" (I Timothy 2:5).

God's plan is easily understood. Romans 6:23 declares, "The wages of sin is death", but Someone had to pay.

Jesus paid the price. The gift of God is eternal life through Him. The veil of the temple was torn from top to bottom. Jesus qualified. He was the first born, spotless Son of God. He died that I might live. He lives that I might have eternal life. Christ's position now is one of an advocate! He is seated at the right hand of God and He is making intercession for us. I can never approach a Holy God as a sinful man—my righteousness is as filthy rags before Him! The only way that I can secure Christ as my advocate or attorney is to meet Him at an altar of prayer and ask Him to represent me.

Accept His salvation and in so doing begin an abundant life here and an eternity with Christ. We have heard the joyful sound—Jesus saves!

Change Sides

If we're going to seek first the kingdom of God, we need to know what the Kingdom of God is. What does it mean to us. How do we define it or describe it? In His end-time discussion in Matthew 24:14, Jesus said, "And this Gospel of the Kingdom will be preached in all the world as a witness to all the nations, and then the end will come."

What is the Gospel of the Kingdom of God? And what is the Kingdom of God? Is it past, or present or future? Yes! Some say it's only future—that we're promised a future—but we're on our own in the present.

Since recorded history, men have been trying to form an ideal society. Plato, from ancient Greece, dreamed of an ideal society based on an ethical political framework. Some tried to copy his ideas but Plato learned that political and social philosophies could never bring about what his soul craved. Augustine believed that the kingdom of God was the church. Calvin agreed in part, but not totally. Calvin believed the kingdom of God was the true church, the invisible church that was within the visible church. This church would, by preaching the Gospel of the kingdom, so change the lives of men and women and nations that things would get better and better until a point in history when the earth would proclaim Jesus as Lord and King. At this point Jesus would return to earth and accept the Kingdom.

Here are some basic Biblical principles that must be put into the mix. The Kingdom of God is not only future but present as well. Romans 14:17, "For the Kingdom of God is not meat and drink, but righteousness, peace and joy in the Holy Spirit." In other words, the natural blends with the supernatural causing a person to be able to experience the Fruit of the Spirit. If you associate with the Holy Spirit, it will rub off on you. The natural result will be a way of life that has a God quality that goes beyond the routine of meat and drink.

If you can picture a football game—each team at the opposite end of the field—one team represents the kingdom of darkness, the other represents the kingdom of God. During the game, one of the main players of the darkness team takes off his shirt and number then goes out on the field and plays on the Kingdom of God team. He simply switches sides.

That's what happens to us. We literally switch teams. There are some that try to stay neutral- like the civil war soldier who wore a gray shirt and blue pants. Both sides shot at him.

Satan's kingdom is only temporary. Christ's authority has no ending. Satan's time is growing short. God is in complete control and we are on the victorious side! There's a famine today of hearing the Good News. We hear what Satan is doing and what politicians are doing. Let's hear Good News. The Gospel of the Kingdom has to be heard, experienced and then proclaimed. The kingdom is not of this world, but it affects this world.

It means changing teams. Taking off the uniform of the Prince of Darkness and coming over on the side of the King of Kings. What are you waiting for?

How About Your Heart

There's a lot in the Bible about the condition of our hearts before God. The Lord looks on the heart. He knows our hearts. We can tell how men look. But God can tell what they are! He sees the thoughts and intents and judges men by what He sees. That's why we must leave the decisions and the final audit in His hands.

In I Samuel 28:15 there's a sad commentary on the life of the Great King Saul of Israel. "The Lord hath taken the Kingdom of Israel from you this day" The Lord is the final word. Saul had made his choices against the direct Word of the Lord—and lost! You always do.

There's a unique contract recorded in these chapters of the Bible. Not many years before this story Samuel was again choosing a King—or looking for God's choice of a King—and the Lord had chosen Saul the King of Kish. Saul was a magnificent looking person. Chapter 10:23, says he was higher than all of the others from his shoulders up. His outward appearance was one of excellence. He even looked like the man for the job! As long as he kept his heart right before God, he *was* the man for the job. God's anointing was upon Saul, but something happened. It's sad, but it happens too often.

In verse 26 of Chapter 15 the Word says, "Thou hast rejected the Lord—and the Lord hath rejected thee!" Saul was still impressive in his outward appearance, but his heart was changed. God looks on our hearts and is totally unimpressed by our looks.

The Lord doesn't see us as we see. Our vision is limited to outward appearance. We have a pre-recorded idea of what we expect. We judge by what they wear, how they look, what they drive. God is interested in our hearts!

What does God see in your heart today? He knows our secrets. He knew what was in David. David wasn't perfect but his heart was bent toward God!

Mark 7:21, "From within, out of the heart of men proceed evil thoughts, adultery, fornication, murder," etc. We can't see these things in a person's heart, but God does! The heart is the center of life.

If there's not much of Christ in our heart, there can't be much of Him in our conversation. If He is in our heart as the center or our love, our conversation will be centered in Him. Jesus is in the heart transplant business. He's looking into our lives and checking for heart disease. Can you pray with David in Psalm 51, "Create in me a clean heart" and "restore to me the joy of my salvation". If life has lost its meaning, let Him do a heart transplant in you.

God's Way or No Way

A visitor to Yellowstone National Park was watching some Grizzly bears eating. The guide told the observers that the Grizzly Bear is the king of the beasts in the west; overpowered only by it's northern cousin the Kodiak Brown bear. When a Grizzly is eating, no one or no animal dares to bother him. Later the tourist noticed that there was one animal that was permitted to eat with the bear. It was a common skunk. The bear could have easily wasted the skunk without any effort whatsoever. He no doubt resented the skunk barging in on his meal but he didn't attack—why? He knew the high cost of getting even! It wouldn't be worth the satisfaction. God help all of us to learn that lesson!

David learned the lesson in Psalm 35. He had encountered a few skunks in his lifetime. People he had befriended and helped turned against him. They falsely accused him. People that he had wept for and cried for cheerfully attacked him—and it hurt. Rejection has a sharp stinger. Psalm 35:7, "Since they hid their net for me without cause and without cause dug a pit for me". Has that ever happened to you? You went out of your way to be kind and were repaid with insult and injury? How did you react? There's some great advice throughout Psalm 35. Verse one is a great place to start. Take it to the Lord! It's easier said than done. We are emotional people. How do we handle it so that God is pleased? David was a good example. He told the Lord how he felt and turned the problem over to God. Lord, YOU contend with those who contend with me, YOU fight against those who fight against me. Can you avoid, like the Grizzly Bear, attacking the skunk? Can you turn it over to God and let Him deal with that person? God will give you the wisdom and the strength to bring about a quick solution.

Are you willing to get the ball rolling? God took the initiative. He loved so much that He gave—so that you and I should not perish! You know the story and the Bible tells us clearly what it cost the Heavenly Father to reach way down for us. I want to challenge you today to continue God's work of restoration to the lost, the fallen, the backslider, even the one who tried to destroy you. Don't wait for someone else to do it. Don't sit around saying I could have or I should have; do it!

Taste and See!

There are many people today who ask the questions: What is life all about? Where are we going? What is our main purpose of being here? Are we just another rung on the evolutionary ladder? Are we one step above the animals as the humanist teaches, or are we just a little lower than the angels as the Bible teaches? Why does life leave me so empty? Many of you will agree that the promises of the "good life", that the world's system is trying so hard to project (through the brainwashing commercials and the media), are not true! How many have tried society's formulas for being happy and being fulfilled and have been left with a very bitter taste? The larger percentage of mankind, from the adolescent to the senior citizen, have believed the lies and the glittering promises—and have found them to be a bubble that bursts! The elusive "good life" disappears. The lower than animal lifestyle, the lust for things and the deceitfulness of riches leave a person empty. The promise is for fullness, but the end result is emptiness! Whether it's gross sin and perversion or whether it's seeking the enlightenment of man-made religion, the answers are still missing.

There's only one place to find truth and life. Jesus said it. "I've proved it." "I am the Way, the Truth, and the Life!" (John 14:6). Life Abundantly!

Pastor, can I find fulfillment today? Can I abound? Is there really satisfaction in life? To answer today's questions like: Why are we here? What is life all about? etc. Paul gives this exhortation: Yes, there is a reason for existing. When that reason is realized and the conditions are met, then life becomes relevant! Life becomes purposeful and the result is true happiness. Man cannot be fulfilled with the same urges that the animal has: food, rest, and multiplying. Man has to go beyond the natural to the supernatural. Man, to be fulfilled, must have a connection with another world!

Let's look at some of the guarantees. Fullness for emptiness, He takes away the emptiness and loneliness. Matthew 28:20, "Lo, I am with you always, even to the end of the age." The world is afraid of the end! With Jesus in your life you are fulfilled—no matter what the circumstances.

He takes away the emptiness of sadness and replaces it with Joy! John 15:11, "These things have I spoken unto you that my Joy might remain in you and that your Joy may be full." His Joy is a supernatural joy! It overcomes tribulation. It laughs at lions. It fears not the fire. It's a tower of strength!

He takes away the emptiness of bondage. He replaces bondage with freedom! Habits break like paper chains when you give Him control of your life. The monotony goes out of life. Things that are now your master become your servant! No chain can hold the soul that is submitted to His freedom!

Finally, He takes away the emptiness of doubt and confusion. He replaces it with blessed assurance! He has a full warehouse of supply.

Haunted By Grandmother's Ghost

Do you believe in Ghosts? I don't believe in those white-sheeted forms that appear and disappear, that move around darkened rooms on wires in the hands of some spiritualist. I don't believe in the ghosts, like the ones in the Christmas story: Christmas past, present and future, etc. We're programmed today by TV cartoons, and sitcoms—even innocent ones like "Highway to Heaven"—to lean in the direction of white magic, or good witches or good ghosts. Nor do I believe in re-incarnation; that we'll come back in another form and live again as a fly or a bee or a roach or a chicken. I believe in being kind to animals, including my web-footed friends, but not because a duck may be somebody's mother! But I do believe my ancestors live on in me! My mother's personality and my father's did not go to the grave with them. Their ways are an integral part of me—my mother's faith will not stop at the grave for it has influenced me. You and I are largely who and what we are because our parents influenced us. That can be good or bad depending on the situation. If it's bad, thank God, He can make it good. It's scary when you think of it, your children will have the same habits that you have in reference to their commitment to God. If you're spasmodic in church attendance, they will be also. If you're careless in your giving to God, they will be as well.

There are some hurdles and barriers that we build for our children that they have a hard time getting over later on in life. Many of you today are haunted by influences of your past. We have choices. We can either use our past as an excuse and vegetate, or we can use our "school of hard knocks" experience as a stepping stone rather than a stumbling block.

We are created with individual choice—no power can control us without our consent. Spiritually speaking, Satan can't control you against your will. When you reach for the TV knob, or the bottle, or the line of coke, or the needle, or the dirty book, there is power available to say NO if you want to. The temptation is there, I Corinthians 10:13 says that it's common to man, but God is faithful—God will help you and will *with that temptation* make a way of escape so that you may be able to bear it.

The same power that wrote the book of Acts is available today. You and I need it in our lives and churches! Paul said, "Keep the faith that has been passed down from former generations", and with that Godly heritage at work in your life you will have the power to become what God planned for you to become. You're not what you wish to be, but what you choose to be.

Have You Been Re-born or Stillborn?

I'm not sure of the exact statistics, but I read that America has over 130,000,000 born-again people resident in this country. I would like to believe that, but if there were truly 130,000,000 born-again believers in America, there would be such a revival of Godliness and morality that America could be cleansed from its sin. Perhaps 130,000,000 have walked an aisle or made a decision or signed a card, but that's not necessarily being "born-again".

What does it really mean to be born-again? Perhaps today the Holy Spirit wants us to do some real inventory—to re-evaluate our own stand—to say, "Am I really a born-again Christian?"

It's 2000 years ago in Jerusalem. The sun has set in the Mediterranean Sea. It's dark and a Jewish religious leader named Nicodemus comes for an interview with Jesus. He is already a believer. You can tell by his opening statement—but he is spiritually lost. Belief for beliefs' sake is not enough! Jesus says, "There must be a Spiritual re-birth in every life!"

The question then arises: Why? You can go back to page one for the answer. Genesis 1 tells us that God determined to create man in His own image—His divine image. So what is the Biblical definition of "image"? Archie Bunker and Meathead had a discussion about this one time; Archie was frustrated by his agnostic son-in-law. "I'm telling you that I was created in the image of God!" Meathead says, "Are you telling me that YOU look like God!?" and Archie replies, "Well, I ain't sayin' you can't tell us apart!" Too many make the mistake of thinking that the Divine Image is something physical. Jesus said that God is a Spirit and we who worship Him do so in Spirit and in truth! When Adam and Eve were created they had inside of them the Spirit of God. That was the Godly image. It had nothing to do with the physical. It was all spiritual! When they disobeyed by eating the forbidden fruit, something happened! The Spirit of God within them died. Their physical bodies lived for a long time but inside they were spiritually dead.

You can make numerous decisions and still be spiritually dead. You can walk church aisles to the altar until you have holes in your shoes. You can sign cards until you get carpel tunnel syndrome—and still be dead. You can weep real tears at the sad stories and feel stirring emotions—and still not be born-again. There has to be a literal new birth inside of you! That birth is when Christ comes to live within you. Paul said it this way in Galatians 2:20, "I live, yet it is not I who lives, but it is Christ who lives (where?) in me! Which is my hope of glory and my reason for living."

We come to God under conviction—we repent—and at that moment the Blood of Christ washes us clean from our past. Jesus literally takes over our lives. He enters with all of His strength, love, tenderness and mercy.

When you're cleansed by the Blood of Christ, old things pass away and all things become new. That's God's promise in His Word—and it's manifested all around you even today. I am blessed every week when I look over the crowd at church and see men and women and teenagers who were desperately lost in sin but who are now saved by His Spirit and living holy and productive lives. This is only brought about by God's regeneration of the human heart!

Second Thoughts

Have you ever done your best and still felt like a failure? Perhaps you've tried for years to win someone to Christ seemingly to no avail. It seemed like you'd given everything that you had and you struck out. Paul was in that place with the Galatians. He was winding down his life's work and felt that he had to make a final challenge. It's a familiar scenario, Mom may have tried all of her life to reach a son or a daughter—now they're standing by her bedside as she's about to go home—and she's searching for words—final words to reach them for Christ. The appeals in Scripture are many and varied. Paul himself had used many appeals to get the job done. He wrote to Timothy, appealing to his common sense in I Timothy 5:8, "Godliness is profitable!" He wrote to the Romans about the reasonableness of a commitment; Romans 12:2, " is your reasonable service". He appealed to their affection in 2 Corinthians 5:14, "The love of Christ constrains us". Paul tried to sound the alarm in Galatians 6:7, "Be not deceived", etc. What more could he say? He preached from history and from experience, he preached Jesus and the cross, he preached out of a personal love and affection for the Galatians—and he won many—but others were hard and full of rejection. Paul could be saying, "I've done all that I can do, but what if it's all in vain?" I've felt that way and so have you.

We see it in the life of Jesus on those last few days on earth—even in His struggle with His Twelve Disciples. Three and a half years He traveled and slept and ate with them. He was friend, teacher, protector and provider. No one spoke like Him or worked as tirelessly as He did. He found them when they were rude, and vulgar, dull and even rebellious, but Jesus poured out His love on them. He turned the lights on. He lifted them and remade them and turned them into mighty men of valor. They became apostles. But it wasn't easy. They forsook Him and fled. Peter cursed and denied, and Judas betrayed him with a kiss. But Jesus still loved him to the end.

We have the power to receive or refuse. We should learn the lessons from history. Nations have refused God for various reasons—they have rebelled against the prophets and the preachers: some out of general rebellion and some out of greed. Back in the mid 1800s our nation faced a dilemma. Many men who fled England because of religious tyranny and to be free of slavery began to see the profit that could be made from cotton. The desire for gold created the need for slaves and you know the rest of the story. One man sitting in the East Room of the While House wept over the direction of the nation. He begged for liberty and for understanding. He pled with the North and the South. Don't separate, brothers. Don't build a wall. He made a final plea: "My Fellow countrymen, we are not enemies but friends. We must not be enemies. Though passion may have strained it we must not break our bonds of affection." It was a powerful plea, but it was all in vain.

God is always close to us. He's pleading with us through messengers and messages. God goes through great effort to bring us to Himself—your life is full of God's reaching out to you. How will the last page of your life read? Is it all in vain? God has not left Himself without a witness. We are inexcusable. An ancient writer wrote these words, "The wrongdoer doesn't need a scourge, a whip, or a dungeon, because that dread avenger, his conscience, is ever with him! Remember—conscience is God's tool. It is God speaking.

God's providence is always before you. You called on God soon enough when you were sick, or when you needed help. You forget Him so soon when you are well. The Lord was necessary when you buried that loved one, but "I'll wait till I need Him again". God interfered

He Did It All For Me

The events that surrounded the last week prior to the death of Jesus are described in all four of the Gospels, each with a different report or different observation. The humiliation that Jesus suffered was almost equal in pain to the actual death on the Cross. He was slapped, He was spit upon, and His beard was ripped from His face. Prior to this, after His arrest, Jesus spent most of the night in a filthy dungeon underneath the house of the high priest. Before daylight He was taken before Pilate who was the Roman appointed governor of Judea. As Jesus stood before Pilate, this hardened man, hardened to the point of little feeling or conscience, was unnerved—partly because of the dream that his wife had and largely because of the awesome presence of this Nazarene. Several times Pilate came to Jesus' defense, and twice he asked for mercy for Jesus. (John 18:38) "I find no fault in Him". And in Chapter 19:7-8 when they told Pilate that Jesus professed to be the Son of God, Pilate was more afraid. The religious people were not afraid. They were blind and bound by tradition and rebellion against God. They were looking for man-made solutions through man-made religion, but this heathen governor was afraid. Anyone who denies the deity of Christ is a fool.

I didn't say that: the Bible says that. Even the devils believe—and they tremble. Jesus calmly stood as Pilate desperately tried to make some sense out of the whole situation. Old Pontius thought that he was the judge, but in fact he was on trial before God's eternal bench.

The familiar story is still awesome; he called for a basin of water to wash away the stain. It takes more than water; it takes blood to wash away the stain of guilt and sin. It was wrong to crucify Jesus and Pilate knew it, and so to please the crowd Pilate had Jesus scourged. This scouring was an experience that is indescribably horrible. They would tie the victim to a post and strip him. His hands were tied on the other side. The only thing that he wore was a leather guard around his neck. The one who held the whip was a man who was skilled in his trade. His skill was to beat a person within inches of his life actually tearing skin and flesh from the back of the accused. They took Jesus to the Public Hall, they placed a crown of thorns on His head, they put a reed in his hand, and they cried the same cry that took place five days earlier, Palm Sunday: "Hail, king of the Jews". The crucifixion was next after Jesus carried the cross on His back—a back that was so much raw flesh—the slivers and splinters torturing Him beyond description. They took the nails

(5″spikes) and drove them through his hands and feet with a wooden mallet and then lifted the cross and dropped it into the hole. Death on the cross came through suffocation. Custom tells us that before the scourging they stripped the victim. That is a shocking statement—they stripped Him. You say, "Pastor, that's horrible! How humiliating to be stripped naked publicly, but I have to tell you that Jesus is still being stripped today! In our seminaries and universities. In our homes, our churches, and ours schools, Jesus is being stripped. He's stripped of His Deity. They say He was a good man and a great teacher, a wonderful humanitarian, but He was not God! To strip Him of His deity, his authority and Lordship is as cruel today as it was in Pilate's hall.

The good news is that Jesus suffered all of this to pay the required penalty for you and for me. Personally, the choice is yours today!

The Difference Between Right and Wrong

It's so obvious to the casual observer that sin is out of control on this planet. It's nothing new. In Genesis 4:7 Moses recorded a conversation between God and Cain. "Sin lies at the door and sin's desire is for you, but you should rule over it!" Sin is always there. You cannot deny it. Deception and fraud in the workplace faces some of you regularly. If sin was not a reality then why do you need an attorney to read a contract before you sign it? Even referees and umpires know the difference between right and wrong. If you'll allow me to be basic and elementary today, I want to show you five facts about sin:

Sin Grows: A child's sin seems so small, but it doesn't remain small. All too soon sin begins to bring bondage. The habit becomes fixed in the body and the brain. Sin begins to dictate and direct actions and reactions.

Sin Deceives: It entices and lures. It says, "Come and sample my delights". Sin promises light and fun fellowship and freedom from rules. It gives darkness, and sorrow, loneliness and bondage. Sin kisses with the kiss of death.

Sin leads to moral insanity: You begin to call wrong right and right wrong. It's like the difference between night and day. Your perception is totally distorted. You don't think right. How can a person who knows the lethal danger of STD's today continue a promiscuous and perverted lifestyle? Because sin makes you morally insane.

Sin Kills: One hole will sink a ship if not repaired. One lie will cause you to be a liar. One drop of poison will cause death.

Sin Marks and Disfigures: It pollutes the mind, the body and the soul! Only sin has this power. Poverty cannot harm the soul. Tragedy cannot harm the soul. Hard times cannot harm the soul. As a matter of fact, these things can beautify the soul. They have a way of building character. Sin cannot build character.

Sin scars and disfigures the real you. It makes you ugly inside. There are no beautiful perverts, or murderers or thieves. You won't find a statue of Ted Bundy gracing our parks. Anger and rage, and uncontrolled tongues damage your life. Sin leaves you unclean. You wallow in the mire. You thrive on pollution.

Ask the alcoholic or the slave to pornography, or the drug addict. Ask them if they feel clean. They know what it feels like to be in torment.

So, what can wash away my sin? Maybe tears will do it! Not hardly! Being sorry brings tears. Being sorry is never enough. Tears will not erase one single sin. What about baptism, Pastor? Surely that counts for something. I wish baptism could wash away sin. There's no cleansing for sin in water. You are just as well off with a vacuum cleaner. Water cleanses the body, but it cannot cleanse the soul. You cannot add anything to the price paid at Calvary.

The good news is this: there's not a spot on my soul that He cannot cleanse and permanently remove. God's total answer to the sin problem is Calvary. His Blood cleanses because He is God's son! My debt was paid by His sacrifice.

"Walk in the Light"—come out into the open before God. He will receive you NOW.

God Is Mercy Full

Ezra was one of the outstanding men of God in the Old Testament. He came by his character honestly. He was a direct descendant of Caleb—one of the 12 spies who went into the land with Joshua. God said of Caleb (Numbers 14:24), "But my servant Caleb, because he hath another spirit and has followed me fully, him will I bring into the land wherein he went, and his seed shall possess it!" Ezra followed in the footsteps of his great grandfather. He is known as the man who honored Scripture, and the man who loved God and God's Word. In Ezra 7:6 the Word says that "He was a ready scribe", or in our words he was well versed in the Law of Moses. Ezra knew the Scriptures not by osmosis or heredity, but by being a student of the Word. Verse 10 tells us Ezra had prepared his heart to seek the law of the Lord and do it—and teach it to Israel. He was a student, an interpreter, a writer, and a very capable administrator. As a man, Ezra was humble, he was trustworthy, he knew how to pray, and had a great burden for his people. He wanted to know the Law and wanted to do the Law. He mourned for the backsliding of his people and would do his best to bring restoration to those whom he was called to minister.

It grieved Ezra that people who called themselves by the name of the Lord would so grossly violate God's Word. Ezra knew the Word of God and he knew how to call sin by its real name, SIN. The sin of his people brought him great sorrow. All day Ezra sat in mourning because of the sin of his people, "And at the evening sacrifice I rose up from my heaviness, fell on my knees, and spread out my hands unto the Lord" (Ezra 9:5) .

In a humble posture, totally bowed before God, Ezra prayed an intercessory prayer for his people, "O God, I blush to lift up my face to Thee."(Ezra 9:6) Ezra confesses the sins of his people and pleads to God for Mercy. "Our sins have grown unto the heavens." Over our heads—we're drowning in our transgressions—but even though their sins reached the heavens as they cried for forgiveness, they found out that their sin ran right into the Mercy of God, for Psalms 36:5 says, "For thy Mercy, Oh Lord, is in the Heavens, and Thy faithfulness reaches to the clouds." Verse 7, "How excellent is thy loving kindness, O Lord!" Praise God for His Mercy! We were bondsmen, but God delivered us through His wonderful Mercy. How foolish to mingle in sin and expose ourselves to God's displeasure. It's as if we drove another nail into Jesus' hands—as if we crucified Christ over again. In Heaven's court we stand guilty, but I have to refer you once again to the great Salvation chapter, Eph. 2:2-5, "In times past we walked according to the course of this world, according to the Prince of the Power of the air, the Spirit that now works in the children of disobedience". But God, who is rich in Mercy, because of His great Love, He does not hold into our account when we follow Ezra's message and come to Him in repentance and come to Him for restoration! , That Mercy comes from God. , It is God who is rich in Mercy!

He will supply all of your need—and you need Mercy. You may not be as loud as Ezra's crowd, you may not be as bad as the thief on the cross, but God's Mercy reached him. In the morning He was with the thieves, that afternoon He associated with the purest of Heaven! Look at the crowd on the day of Pentecost, their hands were dripping with the blood of the Son of God, and Peter said to them, "Whosoever shall call on the Name of the Lord shall be saved!".

God is rich in Mercy—let Him meet your need today! All of your need!

Healthy and Unhealthy Fear

I John 4:18, "There is no fear in love; but perfect love casteth out fear, because fear hath torment. He that feareth is not made perfect in love."

The end of this verse clearly states that fear hath torment. It's like a cancer in your emotions. Fear gnaws at a person. Fear needs to be dealt with right away. There are healthy fears. Fear of fire is a plus; it's healthy. A respectful fear is a positive—I need to respect traffic. Thank God our nuclear people respect atomic power. Respect for rules of the road and respect for authority is what keeps our society going.

There's an Old Testament phrase that is repeated in the Psalms and the Proverbs. Psalm 111:10, "The fear of the Lord is the beginning of Wisdom." We're not talking of an "afraid of" kind of cowardly fear. We're talking about healthy respect! The person who lives as if there is no God or no accountability, the Bible calls a fool. It's worse than playing with fire. Psalms 33:8 says, "Let all the earth fear the Lord; let all the inhabitants of the world stand in awe of Him." That's a healthy fear that leads to safety.

God makes the rules—He is the lawgiver. He insists on obedience. No one escapes His administration. Isaiah 13:11 says, "I will punish the world for their evil, and the wicked for their iniquity; and I will cause the arrogance of the proud to cease, and I will lay low the haughtiness of the terrible." A person who does not keep that thought in mind is a careless person. God said it and He means it. Don't presume on His wonderful mercy.

You can't violate physical laws and go untouched and you can't violate moral laws and it not catch up with you. The facts are the facts. The jury is finished deliberating. The sexual revolution and the free love society sowed to the wind and reaped the whirlwind! Living together outside of marriage destroys people for years to come. Being "sexually" active in your teens causes many hurts for many years. Being morally careless without respect for God and His plan destroys common people as well as princes, and princesses and presidents.

It is a relationship, living in harmony with God, which brings contentment and "casts out fear". You'll never make it any other way.

Working for Caesar Wasn't Easy

This letter to the Philippians was written by Paul when he was a prisoner in Rome. It's not a letter of sorrow or regret, but throughout Paul expresses consecration and love for Christ and His church and spiritual joy. There's a lot of positive thinking in Philippians. Robert Schuler and Norman Vincent Peale were not the originals when it came to being positive. As I read and studied this letter, I was fascinated by 4:22, "All the saints in Rome salute you Chiefly they of Caesar's household!" Is it really possible to be a saint in Caesar's household?

In order to fully appreciate this verse of Scripture we need to understand several things: What is a saint? How can a sinner become a saint? Is it possible to remain a saint in hard places?

What is a saint? Webster defines it as "one of God's chosen." A saint is not necessarily one that has been canonized by the church or one who has earned sainthood. A saint is a disciple of Christ who has accepted or received Christ in their heart and turned their life over to Him. Paul began all his letters by addressing the saints and the faithful. One of Paul's favorite descriptions of a Christian is, one who is "in Christ". To be in Christ was to make you a new creation—from an ain't to a saint.

How does a person make the transition from a sinner to a saint? Anyone can be a saint, but there's only one way to get there. That's through the Savior. It works in the reverse as well. When a child of God is tempted to go back to sin, the Savior stands in between, and does His best to bring him back to the right path. He's a personal Savior! You and I have a tremendous privilege as a Christian. What thrilled me most about this passage of Scripture though was the environment for these saints. They were believers, men and women "in Christ" in Caesar's household. Who would expect to find them there? But as you grow in God and meet more and more of the family, you realize that it's possible to serve God in any circumstance.

This is the strongest argument I can give to the complainer who is always defeated. You hear it often in the ministry, "I can't be a Christian in the surroundings where I work or live." Yes you can! None of us are in surroundings that are totally helpful. I know it's not easy, you that work in the office where immorality and partying are acceptable practices. This Caesar that Paul refers to was the dreaded Nero. Nero was a black spot even in the corrupt history of Rome. Can you imagine keeping mind and body clean in a place where every form of filth was encouraged? It takes moral backbone.

It takes a discovery of inner resources. There are resources available to us. When there's nothing outward to encourage you, there's everything inward to strengthen you. In the book, *Dying We Live,* published letters from a Nazi prison camp, Ludwig Steil who died in Dachau in 1945 wrote these words, "During the night the verse of the hymn, when all my strength was shattered, I felt the helping hand." Those words kept running through my mind and I thanked God for the advantage that we Christians have in prison over those who have no hope." A Christian is never at the mercy of circumstances.

Your victory in Caesar's household will affect others. Your life counts far more than you realize.

Don't Let Fear Overwhelm You

The Apostle Paul had discernment and he knew what the early Christians would be going through. Hardships and warfare like never before! The only real victory would come through the Lord's strength.

Paul knew that a soul that was bound by fear and focused with their present trials would be hard to get through to. Fear is a de-mobilizer. Fear will cause you to fail! These are fearful days. These are days in which Satan would love to render the Christian and the church ineffective. Paul knew the danger of fear. He wrote, "Fightings and fears within and without!" We're there today. The inward attacks of the enemy and the troublesome world situation can easily cause fear to control your mind! Don't let your fears overwhelm you! Take courage. Be strong IN THE LORD. The final outcome will not rest on your skill or your strength. The outcome rests in God's performance. Let your strength be in the Lord. Fear will attack you. Fear chased Elijah to the wilderness to hide. Fear haunted David, but David knew where to turn. Psalm 56:2-3 says, "My enemies are fearsome. They would swallow me up, but when fear comes, I will trust in thee." In God will I praise and in God will I put my trust!

Be strong in the Lord! How? Here's how. The Old Testament frequently exhorts the believer to be strong. 2 Chronicles 32:7 says, "Be strong and courageous" Isaiah 35:4 says to them of a fearful heart "Be strong!" It's possible to be strong in the 2000s? The challenge cannot be met unless you have help from a higher source than yourself. There is a main line that comes from God and that line is prayer. The Christian on his knees is a posture that puts fear into the enemy. The world will laugh. The carnal, weak Christian has no time, but the one who wants to be strong in the Lord *will be* as you approach God and tap into His strength.

"Head" knowledge is not enough. Following Christ is a matter of the heart. Your heart must be fixed. If not, then your principles, your motives, no matter how good they may be will not hold up in battle. They will be as useful as a gun without bullets. It will make a good club but won't last too long against live ammunition.

Have You Come Out of the Closet?

To be a disciple of Christ is the greatest privilege on earth. Nothing else can compare with it. If you are a disciple, what kind of a disciple are you? The Bible tells us of those who were open and unashamed like Paul who wrote to the Roman Church in 1:16, "I am not ashamed..." Then there were those who were ashamed—or secret disciples. Just as in Jesus' day we have both kinds today. When Jesus preached, he reached all types of people in His congregation.

Often there was a man in the crowd, a man who was a believer, but not in a hurry to become public with his confession of faith. Joseph of Arimathea did not like publicity. At one time in his life he had heard the life changing message from one of the Lord's dynamic sermons. He went home and dug out the old scrolls where the Scriptures were recorded, and through reading he became convinced that Christ was the Messiah. The tragedy was that he remained a secret disciple. It would be interesting to talk to Joseph and ask him why he was afraid to tell people of his newly found faith in Christ. Why keep it so hush-hush? There are many answers that Joseph could have given, and there are several that are still used today—mostly by people like Joseph whose character was as good as his upbringing. He may have said, "I'm naturally backward and too timid to be an all-out Christian. I can't get myself to be on display in a conversation, especially in religious matters."

We can't hide behind our disposition. Who cares what men may say about our stand for the Lord? In Mark 8:38, Jesus said, "Who ever shall be ashamed of Me and My word, I'll be ashamed of him."

Joseph came to that day of decision on one Friday afternoon. He stood off in the crowd unnoticed, yet eagerly watching every detail. He had seen the unfair trial of the Lord. He had heard the murderous scheming. He knew that the whole scene was far from right. Joseph followed to the hill called Calvary and heard the hammer drive the nails through the hands that were instruments of healing, love, and miracles to rich and poor alike.

The hands that touched blind eyes, that lifted the lame, that set the captive free, that blessed the little children and that broke the bread. He heard the hammer drive the nails and it did something in Joseph! He couldn't stand there and watch his beloved Lord agonize and die like a common criminal. It took a clear vision of the cross to change this secret disciple into a bold fearless one.

Friend, if you're only a secret disciple, then you need another look at Calvary's cross. You need to see the crown of thorns oozing blood. You need to see again the pain on His face. You need to see His body jolted as the cross is put into place. You need to see the love in that sacred head as He looks in your direction. Joseph saw Him hanging between Heaven and Earth for him. No man can see the crucified Christ and remain a secret disciple. It's impossible.

Joseph was never the same man again. Calvary changed him completely. Go to the cross and see what Jesus did for you and you'll never be a secret disciple again.

Discipleship Isn't Free

I Corinthians 9:24 reads like this in the Living Bible: *"In a race everyone runs but only one person gets first prize, so run your race to win!"* Paul was a survivor—more than that, he was a winner. He proved it over and over again. When he and Silas were holding their first-ever European meeting in a place called Philippi they ended up in a filthy Philippian jail—beaten, bleeding, and broken—all of their hopes smashed. They had gone to that city full of hope. They were led by the Spirit of God. They had invaded Europe for the Lord Jesus Christ. They had instant results (Acts 16:13-15), and immediately Satan went to work to stop the Gospel. A demon possessed girl began to follow them and she would shout "These men are servants of the most high God! They've come to tell you how to have your sins forgiven!" After several days Paul had enough and cast the demon out of her with one command! He and Silas were grabbed, arrested, tried, found guilty, beaten with clubs and rods, and thrown into a filthy jail! What started out as a great crusade for Christ was over! By human standards they were done; but were they? No way! You and I know the end of the story. God had not deserted them. There was tremendous victory rather than defeat. They found they were not alone. No matter what the test He will not fail you! Look at what they did. They prayed and sang praises to the Lord. It takes that to be a winner. Complaining, moaning, blaming someone else or God, bitterness—that's the way of the loser. It does not help. Praying helps! They prayed and they sang. Anyone can sing when the sun is shining bright, but a winner has a song in his heart at night! There's a formula to being a winner. All sports fans remember Vince Lombardi. One of his famous quotes was "If winning isn't important, then why do we keep score?" Winning isn't everything—it's the only thing. Paul wasn't talking about games here; he was talking about the game of life: the game that is played for keeps. In your and my spiritual life, winning is the only thing! The cares of this world, the temporary, must fall far behind the eternal. Run your race to win! Every contestant in a race knows that it take pain to win. Your lungs burst, your heart beats, your muscles throb. It takes discipline and training. It's not easy to win—but it is necessary!

To win the race you must run to win, and do whatever you must to lighten up. And as you're running, keep your eyes on the prize. Looking unto Jesus, the author and finisher of our Faith!

Look to Him. Begin tapping in on His Power! You'll find that you can keep going long after others have dropped out! Salvation is free. It's a gift. But discipleship is expensive. It's a commitment to do the will of the Father.

The Scarlet Thread

The story of Rahab and her family in Joshua 2 is a fascinating bit of Scripture. It's about a woman of the trade engaged in a Godless sinful business who receives the Mercy of God. The Mercy of God reaches way down. Rahab was an Old Testament Mary Magdalene. Another lost broken woman who met mercy face to face and was lifted—elevated—to being an heir of God. A joint heir with Jesus Christ from being a servant: a slave of Satan. The thread that Rahab put in the window represents the Blood of Christ. There's a cleansing flow that anyone can plunge into to be clean! There is no other cleansing agent that works to cleanse from sin! Water doesn't do it. Oil doesn't do it. Fire doesn't do it. Without the shedding of Blood, there is NO remission! Jesus came into this world to SAVE sinners. The significance of Blood as a cleansing agent applies both physically and spiritually. If you stop the blood supply in your arm and continue to use that arm—hammer a nail, cut with the scissors, anything that uses the muscles—in just a few seconds you will experience severe pain. Your muscles will cramp and the pain will overwhelm you. When you release the pressure and the blood rushes into your arm, a soothing relief floods the muscles. The pain came because you continued to use the muscles when there was no blood supply. As the muscles converted the oxygen into energy, certain waste products were produced called metabolites. These would normally have been flushed away in the blood stream, but because the blood stream was cut off they produced agony. They were not cleansed by the blood. Normally the blood stream takes care of the waste, but when they accumulated in the blood stream they hurt. The flow of blood cleansed the cells—and the flow of Blood from Calvary cleanses the Soul. Sin is a perpetual problem. It's an anti-body in our system that can only be cleansed by the Blood of the Lamb.

I'm glad that we have access to the overcoming Power of the Blood of Christ! Jesus overcame evil by absorbing it—taking it upon Himself and finally destroying it. He became sin for us!

There are young people today who are being tempted and enticed by Satan's bait. They don't realize that there's a hook hidden the lights and the music, the pleasure and the fun. In the end it bites like a poisonous snake—and it's totally fatal!

Sin damages your life. It disfigures the real you. It leaves you dirty and unclean! Sin is the only thing that will destroy the soul! You may be poor, but poverty cannot harm your soul. Torture or martyrdom doesn't harm the soul. In fact, these things have a way of beautifying the inner person, but sin destroys and leaves an ugly mark! That's why we need the Blood. It cleanses. It covers. It liberates and sets us free!

Why not let Him set you free today?

What Happened Between the Manger and the Cross?

It is the custom in many churches to recite the Apostles Creed in every service. The second paragraph states "who was conceived of the Holy Spirit, born of the Virgin Mary, suffered under Pontius Pilate, was crucified, died, and was buried", etc. The 33 years of Jesus' life are too important to skip over. It would be hard to describe the life of Jesus in just a few words. He was not the Hollywood stereotype or the Prozac Jesus, but one who had so much charisma that people would sit for three days without food just to hear Him speak.

He showed sympathy for a person with leprosy, He was excited over the success of His disciples, He grieved over a sinful city and He cried out in horrible anguish in the Garden. He was a man who could cry. Three times He cried in front of His disciples. He made Himself vulnerable. Jesus loved to praise other people. He said things like, "Your faith has healed you", and "A true Israelite in whom there is no guile". He said of John the Baptist, "There was none greater who is born of women." (Luke 7:28) Peter was "the Rock", and of a cringing woman who displayed a very expensive act of devotion, he said that the story of her generosity will be told forever. Jesus drew people out in a beautiful way. He got them to trust Him. He was available! I don't think that Jesus ever made a list of "things I gotta do today!" He let Himself get distracted by anyone who had a real need. He had time for a hemorrhaging woman and a blind beggar who made a nuisance of himself. He had friends among the elite: Roman Centurions, Pharisees, rich people, prostitutes, and leprosy victims. People liked to be where Jesus was! Where He was there was joy!

His style of teaching was unique: Parables, teaching deep truths through every day happenings. "A man is mugged and left for dead by robbers. A scolding Jewish momma wears down the patience of a judge, a single woman who loses a penny acts as if she lost everything, etc." (Luke 15) The parables produced the desired results.

John said that Jesus came "full of Grace and Truth". Grace—a simple message of God's love. Today, just as in Jesus' day, the crowds are made up of the same components. In the outer circle are the curiosity seekers who are trying to figure Him out. A little bit upset that He is so popular yet afraid to overtly persecute Him for that very reason. Closer in are those who are sincere followers. John's disciples complained that "everyone" was going over to Jesus. Jesus always directed most of His comments to the serious seekers. He pushes them to a deeper level of commitment saying things like: you can't serve two masters, forsake the love of money and worldly pleasures, deny yourself, serve others, and take up your cross. The statements that He made in the Sermon on the Mount are the heart of His message. Here He gave the multitudes His philosophy of life.

If I could give you any advice that will serve you better than anything else, it is to learn to live by His example. The beatitudes are actually promises. Those who mourn will be comforted. Those who are hungry will be filled. The pure in heart will see God. These are promises that Jesus has the authority to make. In a comfortable world it's hard to identify with the Sermon on the Mount. In spite of the philosophy of today, the man who dies with the most toys does not win!

He Will Deliver

In Webster's dictionary *deliverance* is defined as the act of being set free. In our day today, there are many who need to be set free, to be delivered. We're not following some myth or some maybe so, but we're serving the only One who can deliver. He's in the deliverance business. The same God who delivered Noah and his family from the flood, the same God who delivered Joseph from the pit to the palace, the same God who delivered the children of Israel out of bondage, who parted the Red Sea, who brought them into the promised land, delivered the three Hebrew children, spared Daniel from the Lions, set Peter free from prison, delivered Lazarus from the grave (and we could go on and on) is still delivering men from the oppressor!

The setting is ancient Babylon, at approximately 600 BCE. Babylon was the world's leading power in that day. In about 626 BCE a powerful leader named Nebuchadnezzar gained control of the city, and began to rebuild it after it had been devastated by Assyria, under the leadership of Sennacherib in 689 BCE. Nebuchadnezzar had a son who took over the reigns from his father and led the city into world leadership and the height of splendor.

You could read the life story of King Nebuchadnezzar for days and not be bored. He was a military genius as well as a man with classy taste when it came to culture. When he sent his armies out to conquer, he always instructed them to bring back the best of the young men as captives: artists, craftsmen, and wise counselors. In 605 BCE Babylon decided to occupy southern Palestine. They planned their strategy and in 597 BCE Babylon attacked Judah. They took many captives back home from this victory, among whom were Daniel, Hananiah, Mishael, and Azariah. Their names were changed to Belteshazzar, Shadrach, Meshach, and Abednego. Their names were changed, then Nebuchadnezzar tried to change their diet and ultimately tried to get them to forget their God Jehovah, and serve the God of Babylon whose name was Baal. His intention was to de-Israelize them and pro-Babylonianize them all at the same time. In this particular case, Nebuchadnezzar bit off more than he could chew. He had not figured on the faith of these men of God. They were fanatics! He had put them in leadership positions because of their ability and loyalty. They lived well and had great favor with the king, but they refused to disobey God's laws. They refused to become idol worshippers! That's why in the face of all odds against them they found deliverance. I need to hear that because more and more of this world is in direct defiance of God. There are more cults, more self-glorifying preachers, and so many organizations dedicated to anti-God and humanism than ever before, and we cannot afford to bow to them.

There was nothing the three could do about the king's rules. Obey and lose your soul or disobey and lose your life. It was either/or—and they chose or. They put their entire future in God's hand. They believed in deliverance!

We need deliverance for the parents who cannot relate to their teenager, and refuse to try! We need deliverance for the believer who is still bound by habits and actions and thoughts that are not becoming to the child of God. We need deliverance for the Christian who suffers under condemnation and guilt of the past, which render them ineffective. We need deliverance for the believer who lives by feeling alone and has not learned the faith walk. We need deliverance for the person who has never found the release of genuine love for people. We need deliverance for the believer who has never found the freedom of forgiving those who have wronged them. No matter how great the circumstances or how strong the bondage, God is able to deliver you!

Excuses

There's an oriental fable that tells of a man who went to borrow a neighbor's rope. The neighbor said, "I need it to tie up a pile of sand". "But you can't tie sand with a rope!" "Oh yes," said the neighbor, "you can do almost anything with a rope if you don't want to lend it."

Someone said an excuse is "a skin of a reason stuffed with a lie". Making excuses started with Adam "the woman that you gave me". It's her fault. Eve blamed the serpent. It's always easy to blame someone else! It's a human trait. Pass the buck on someone else if you can, but when we stand before God we'll find that the buck stops here.

In Luke 14: 15-24 Jesus told about excuses. The story must have brought smiles to the faces of the hearers, but the message was and is very clear.

The man threw a big party, invited a lot of people and was offered the weakest excuses.

Guest number one said, "I have bought a piece of ground, and I must go and see it. I pray they have me excused". How absurd! Could you believe that a Jewish businessman would buy a piece of ground without seeing it! And even if he did, the land wasn't going anywhere.

Guest number two said, "I have brought 10 oxen and I have to try them out". What difference if he waited till after the party was over—even if it was an all day affair. It takes longer that that to train those oxen. What a weak excuse.

Guest number three said, "I have married a wife and I can't wait to come". I don't think I would have used that one. He was the original "Henpecked Harry". My wife won't let me come! Either he was ashamed to bring her to the feast or he was using her as an excuse because he didn't want to go. If there's one place a bride wants to go it's to a party—a banquet where the servants do all the cooking, serving and clean up!

We've been invited to a party such as human history has never known. Revelation 19:9 calls it the Marriage Supper of the Lamb. God has sent out the invitation to multiplied millions to be part of the great company of the redeemed. But millions have turned down the invitation by offering all kinds of excuses like: "I'll come later, but not now. I have plenty of time". "I'm too sinful—there's no hope for me". Here's a dangerous one: "I'm good enough. I'm as good as the next person". "There are too many hypocrites in the church". And lastly, "I don't understand the Gospel".

There aren't even enough crutches for all of the excuses that we hear. When you stand before God you will not have any crutch to lean on, or anyone else to blame. Every excuse will dissolve in His presence. Every word of self-defense will perish before it is spoken.

You have an invitation to a Gospel Feast. Get rid of the excuses. Prepare to stand whole and clean in God's presence. Lean on Jesus. He's the only one who can speak for you on that day.

Forgiveness is Precious

Remember the old spiritual "It's me, It's me, O Lord" not my brother, or sister or preacher, etc. David didn't write that, but he would like it. He often made those kinds of statements. David knew what it was to fail and fall—and he also knew what it was to forgive and be forgiven. Psalm 32 is a psalm or song of repentance. David had made peace with God! David had sinned grossly—he had willfully and knowingly transgressed God's law. He had tried to cover it for 12 months long. *It's hard to find a more miserable person than the one who is under conviction and yet refuses to turn totally to God,* refuses to confess. It's a pre-requisite. "If we confess our sins He is faithful and just to forgive us and to cleanse us." (I John 1:9) It is in 2 Samuel 12 that Nathan, the prophet, faces David with his sin—His sin of taking another man's wife and having her husband killed. After telling the story in the third person, Nathan asked David for an opinion, "What should happen to such a man?" David's anger was kindled, "The man deserves to die!" (verse 5) Nathan said, "Thou art the man!" and David said in verse 13, "I have sinned before the Lord", not "I couldn't help myself", "God understands my needs" or "Others have done worse than that". No, he said, "I have sinned before the Lord!" He wrote it "I humbly acknowledge my transgression." "Against thee have I sinned", and Nathan replied, "The Lord hath put away thy sin". When David repented God forgave at once! There were consequences—serious ones. "You've given the enemy occasion to blaspheme and they do and will do!" But God's forgiveness was real. David found the fountain open for all sin and uncleanness. It was at this time that David wrote Psalm 32, "Blessed," not a surface blessing—but ecstatically happy, "is the man whose sins are forgiven!"

David, through the Holy Spirit anointing, had a way with words. You could tell that he was rejoicing, that he was free, and that his sins were gone. He uses the word *selah;* a musical term, meaning 'lift up—bring it up to a crescendo!' It's something to praise the Lord for! David uses three words here in the first two verses that merit some study: transgression, sin, and iniquity! And he uses three different words to describe God's dealings concerning all three: forgiven, covered, and imputed not. Transgression means stepping across, one who willfully crosses the line into forbidden territory, and does what he shouldn't do. Sin means to miss the mark. God has a set standard. To sin is to come short of that mark! That's why God intervened and sent Christ to this earth to save sinners! Iniquity infers a lifestyle of wrong. What is the remedy for stepping across, missing the mark, and perversion? What's the Good News? Behold the Lamb of God who TAKES AWAY. He was wounded for my transgressions. They are forgiven—Paid in full! Then my sin is covered. You can't cover your own sins. Some have tried, tried to do things to get God to forget or to turn the other way. Proverbs 28, "He that covereth his sins will not prosper, but who confesseth them shall find mercy!" If we confess, He is faithful and just to forgive and cleanse. When I come to Christ, when I truly repent and cross back over the line and receive forgiveness and cleansing, He doesn't count all of those sins against me anymore! He took it all and paid for it all. The old account is settled and I step out in newness of life.

A Fair Weather Warning

When our sophisticated weather equipment spots the making of a dangerous storm, an elaborate tracking network goes into operation. As they follow the storm three stages of progress are mentioned: a hurricane alert, a hurricane watch, and a hurricane warning. When the warning comes, people begin to evacuate to higher ground to weather out the storm. I have a spiritual weather report for you today.

Many bad trips start with a "soft breeze" and wrong motivations. The sailors wanted to end up for the winter in a more "commodious" port (Acts 27:12) a place of ease and comfort, a place of fun and games. They took chances that went against common sense rules of seamanship. "It can't happen to me" is often the sad response of temptation.

Life is full of snares, verse Luke12:19. The rich farmer said, "I have much goods laid up". Things are going well. I am prospering. Take it easy. Eat, drink, and be merry, for the weather is fair. Jesus said in verse 21 that those who lay up treasures for themselves are fools. If you are concerned about material gain more than spiritual gain, you're off balance. God is not against prosperity, but He wants us to be concerned about being rich toward God. Be careful when prosperity and ease are predicting fair weather. Proverbs 27:1 states, "Don't boast about tomorrow for you know not what a day may bring." The preacher is not the local wet blanket, but He has a handle on heavenly forecasts. Some may be in touch with history and politics, but the man of God must be in touch with Heaven.

Young people are fooled today. Instead of taking the safe way and building character, they want to get going and enjoy the trip with not much thought about the destination. Even though we're in the most educated period in history, our youth are least prepared for life. All of today's experts predict fair weather. "Go for it" is the slogan of the day. Planned Parenthood makes it easy to get rid of the evidence, and casual morals are the order of the day. Young people in their pre-teen years are pressured into adult styles and liberated living, and they're deluded into thinking that the perverted styles of today are the norm.

Jesus called His generation and ours, "blind leaders of the blind" in Matthew 15:14. It's dangerous to deny there are storms, and so no preparation for them. When a shipbuilder builds a ship, he doesn't build it for the calmest weather. He builds the ship to face the fury of the storm. How will it hold up under stress?

Don't be fooled by surface winds and calm weather. The easy way always seems to call. It's different when the storm strikes. Suddenly you need something solid to bring you through. Satan would love to add you to the list of shipwrecks.

You may feel that you can do without God now, but what will you lean on when the struggle comes. We need to learn to learn even in the fair weather times. The Titanic is a perfect example that history affords us. Unsinkable? Not hardly. The party soon turned sour and the band played "Nearer my God to Thee". It's amazing how that you think of God when trouble comes.

If you heed the warning in fair weather—if you let Him guide you in all your ways—if you learn to lean on Jesus, then when you're in your worst storm you'll hear Him say as He did in Matthew 4:27, "Be of good cheer, it is I—be not afraid!"

The Rider of the Pale Horse

William Saragon said, "The best part of man stays forever". He died in May 1980 after a 2 year battle with cancer. Five days before he died, he phoned the Associated Press and made this statement, " Everybody has got to die. I always believed an exception would be made in my case —now what?"

When the Pale Horse rides in, no one can challenge him. No one can knock him out of the saddle. In Revelation 6 we have a description of four horses with their individual riders. The white horse: a conquering hero; the red horse: war; the black horse: famine, and the pale horse: death. And Hell followed him. We've been familiar with this horseman for a long time. It's an encounter that we would like to postpone, put off as long as possible, but we must face it.

Death is an adversary. It tramples you. It's a sniper's bullet, a runaway truck, an exploding airplane, a tornado, or a fire that allows no way of escape. Death rides and is riding towards all of us. Death has a color, "pale". Job knew that color. Job 14:20, "Thou changest his countenance and sendeth him away". Death makes an impression on you that you'll never forget, no doubt about it, so don't be caught by surprise like the above mentioned writer saying, "now what?" Another, H.G. Wells, stated, "If when I die I awaken in another world, I shall be the most surprised person alive." Luther Burbank, a student of nature said, "There is nothing in science that reveals a future life. The universe could not contain the souls of men if individual immortality were a reality." Poor Luther!

Let's read on about this rider. "His name is death and Hell follows with him." So death does not end it all. There is something to follow. The jail follows the sheriff. Death is not the end. "Hell followed with him". The end is not the comfortable casket surrounded by expensive flowers. Hebrews 9:27, "It is appointed after this, the judgment." The grave is just an entrance. Many will face the Hell they laughed at. "Now What?" The pale horse rider is too swift for you to outrun. He will make you face eternity. You refused while you were alive, now you must! "Hell followed with him." The answer to the question "now what?" must be addressed before death rides in! Think about it; it's your life. Do you want to blow it all in a few undisciplined years, years when you indulged like an animal? The entertainment world—the MTV world strongly influences you to "live it up"! Read the headlines: The End Thereof Are the Ways of Death! Those wasted years will be years of deep regret! You'll come to your senses too late with too little. Let's make our time count for eternity.

Time takes my hearing, my recall, my eyesight, etc. But time cannot take away my character! Age can't destroy it. What I am I will take into eternity. My aim is not to take laziness, jealousy, gossip, and carelessness. The outward manifestations of the inward man are renewed day by day!

I'm not running away from the pale horse, I know where I'm going. No devil in Hell can scare a man or woman who is ready to go! When I see an exit sign, I am reminded of Job's question, "If a man dies, will he live again?" Job 14:14. Yes! Job answered it 19:25-27, "I know that my Redeemer lives and He shall stand at last on the Earth, and after my skin is destroyed, I know that my flesh shall see God!"

Mr. Saragon found out too late. He was going somewhere just as you and I! The question is—where?

Do You Lie About Your Weight?

We live in a weight conscious society. Definitely more than any other country in the world our nation holds the record for overweight people, and many are not exactly accurate about their total poundage! I want to talk to you today about God's scales. The final and last word about your weight spiritually must come from Him.

Here's the setting: Nebuchadnezzar ruled over Babylon for 43 years and according to the Word of God there is strong evidence that he died as a believer (read Daniel 4:37). Nebuchadnezzar knew what he was talking about! The last king of Babylon was Nabonidus, Nebuchadnezzar's son-in-law. He made his son Belshazzar his associate. The city was under siege from the Medes and the Persians. They wanted to overrule Babylon and have world dominion. Belshazzar was put in charge of the defense department. Belshazzar was totally bankrupt when it came to morals. He had none. He decided to give a celebration—an anniversary bash for one of the gods that he worshipped. No one thought of danger. No one thought of tomorrow. Who cares? The Medes and

Persians were battering the wall for 48 months. Four years. Our city is unbeatable. They drank wine and praised the gods of gold, silver, brass, iron, wood, and stone! Belshazzar challenged his lords to outdrink him. He was brave in his drunken state. Brave enough to dare God. May I tell you today that others have tried—and there are no survivors! Belshazzar led the way. He lifted a temple vessel to toast the gods of the flesh. They praised the gods of Babylon—and it was his last mistake. Sobriety never came as quickly as it did in that great hall. They saw the fingers of a man holding a pen. Not the wrist or the hand—just the fingers. A Super Power was present. Every drunken eye followed the writing. Then the fingers vanished and only the writing remained.

They called the 80-year-old prophet Daniel. Daniel stood before a shaking king and Daniel read God's Word! He knew his father's writing. Numbered. Weighed. Wanting. It was the sentence of the judge. No appeal. In minutes Belshazzar was dead.

You may carry a lot of weight at the bank or the club or even within your church family, but how do you weigh on God's scale? It's a human condition to minimize our faults and overestimate our good points.

We tip the scales in *our own* favor, " I'm good enough. I'm better than most," and it's self-deceit. It's a false weight and we know it!

If every minister of every church would end up a drunkard, or and adulterer, or a murderer or a child abuser, your chances at the judgment throne of God will not improve by one fraction. You cannot deceive the one who wrote on the wall. God's scales are honest scales. They are balanced on truth. They are very sensitive: weighing thoughts and motives, impulses and intentions. You'll be weighed against your conscience. You'll be weighed against your knowledge. Knowledge is available—there's a church nearby and a Bible in every hotel room!

Today we see more than the fingers, we see the entire Hand reaching toward us. It is recognizable because it has a nail print. It reaches for me and not against me! One drop of Blood from that Hand balanced the scales in my favor!

The enemy of our soul is out to get us. There's no doubt that he desires to steal, kill and destroy—and his destructive force is causing the church, the body of Christ, to be fragmented, and almost isolated. Notice in Luke 23:42 there's a prayer prayed by a thief, "Lord, remember me!" The church today needs to pray this prayer of the thief—", Lord, remember me!"

We can learn much from this thief -perhaps a contemporary of Barabbas. Hanging on one side of Jesus he had a revelation of who Jesus was. On one side there's a condemning voice saying, "If you're really Christ, save yourself and save us. Get us out of here if you're who you think you are!"

On the other side I can almost see the thief turning his head and seeing the agony of Jesus—watching His chest heaving as He tried to keep from suffocating because of the position of His Body on the cross. During the night Jesus had been tortured brutally. His Body was ripped wide open by the whip of the Roman soldier. Words cannot describe the agony that Jesus had endured and it was intensified by the nails and the splinters and the cross.

I can't imagine the horror that kind of death. He would try to stand straight to relieve the pressure on His chest and arms. His back looked like a plowed field, the splinters of the cross caught His ripped flesh. The crown of thorns pressed into His head when He tried to lean His head back, then His lap would give out and buckle throwing the weight of His body on His hands over and over again, twisting to try to relieve the pain. His face is unrecognizable—slapped by 614 soldiers with an open hand, coated with the spit of dozens of townsmen. From the ground up, as we see Him it's unbearable. From the cross down, Jesus knew untold horror as the Father turned His back from the sin that He carried. He was there carrying the sin of the world. He carried AIDS, He paid for the child molester, He bled for the murderer and the adulterer. He was despised and rejected, and He had to hear the one side taunting Him—if you are Christ save yourself and us! He turned to look to the man on the other side.

The thief is saying "Lord". He's calling Him *Lord*! Where did he learn that? Had he heard Jesus preaching somewhere? Had he listened as Pilate questioned Jesus? We don't know. But he knew more than many church people know. He knew more than the chief priests and disciples. He knew that death was a gateway to a new kingdom, a new world. He knew and he makes an unusual request, "Remember me!" or call me to your mind when you come into your Kingdom.

Others have prayed that prayer. Take Samson. Everything had fallen apart. His anointing was gone. His credibility was gone. His reputation was gone. His pride was gone. His eyesight was gone—and he prayed, "Remember me," and God remembered him. His power came back and his victory came back.

The answers came even through the agony that Jesus was suffering. Jesus said, "Assuredly, today you will be with me," Luke23:43. Because of the agony of the Cross, this thief could sing: "Thanks to Calvary, I'm not the man I used to be!"

The Power That Works in Us

It's not in the Bible but it's frequently quoted as Scripture; "God helps those who help themselves." It's been said often and it will be said again—and it can be proven by Scripture even though it's not Biblical. God will not do for us what we can do for ourselves!

The story here is familiar. Lazarus had died. His sisters were grief stricken. He was the only brother. They called on Jesus because He was close to this family. He often visited their home in Bethany for rest and relaxation as well as Martha's cooking.

Lazarus had been dead for four days—lying in the grave. Jesus delayed His visit. He was called while Lazarus was sick. Jesus seemingly allowed the sickness to do its work so that He might strengthen their faith. In John 11:15 He said, "I'm glad for your sakes that I was not there, to the intent that you might believe". The sisters and the disciples needed their faith increased! A beautiful drama was in the making. Jesus asked the question "where have you laid him?" They responded "come and see". Jesus had stopped crying and so had they. Jesus knew that there is only one answer to death—it's the resurrection. "I am the resurrection", He had said—and now He would prove it. When they got to the cemetery, there was a stone. It stood between the dead person and the giver of life! God was ready to do a great work here, but it all hinged on their obedience! Jesus would not remove the stone—they had to do it! We must invest all of the power and energy that we have.

There are some in the grave of alcohol today. Others it's drugs, or gambling, or pornography. They're dead and have been for a long time. How far am I willing to go to help or do I want Jesus to do it all? Will I be involved in reaching into the filth and hopelessness of our generation? God waits to see if I put my shoulder to the stone if I get under the load. It's too late to play church. Nothing will happen in churches that are playing church. Nothing will happen until we want it to happen. It takes more than pity and cursing the darkness and death. It takes more that public crying. The stone has to be removed! Their effort would cause a miracle. Their lack of effort would prevent a miracle! There are stones that cover dead souls, and dead families, and dead cities today!

Martha was quick to mention one hindrance, "Lord, by this time he stinks!" Listen, there's a smell to the death that Satan puts on people. It doesn't take long to find that out! It's a well-established odor.

That's the story of unbelief. "It can't be done. The odds are too great. The game's over." That's what Satan wants you to think. We have to make up our minds! Do you believe that life can replace death? Do you believe the alcoholic can be taken out of the pit? Do you believe the perverted man or woman can be saved? Do you? Then take the first step. Go to them. Help them to see the life giver.

It's never too late when Jesus is there! Forget facts. Forget analysis. The fact is, there will be a stench, but there is a Power available to undo what sin and death and hell have destroyed!

God is serious about what Satan is doing to mankind, to our children, and our teenagers, our singles, and our college kids. I'm here to tell you as Luke said in 19:10, "The Son of man is come to seek and save the lost!" That changes every situation. You roll back the stone and He'll restore the years!

After Death—What?

Appointments are everybody's cross to bear. We all have them: the dentist, the doctor, the barber, the hairdresser, the mechanic, the lawyer, even the taxman. Our lives are directed by appointments. There are good ones and those that we would rather pass by or forget about. We basically control our daily and weekly appointments.

How often have you picked up the phone and changed the time, or perhaps cancelled an appointment? Some of us have even forgotten when we had to meet someone or be somewhere. We've been late and we've been early. It's really our choice. We are in control of our appointment book, but there's one appointment we can't control. "It is appointed unto man once to die and after that the judgment," Hebrews 9:27. We can't postpone it. Some have tried with promises of reform, with offers of money, etc. We can't cancel it. It is appointed. As sure as the sun comes up in the morning that day will come.

I would love to have postponed my father's death and shortly after that my mother's. Selfishly, humanly, I would have if I could, but I couldn't. They had a higher appointment. Kings and presidents can't change it. The fact remains: we have an appointment. It is written and decided and we can't change it.

The appointment of God concerning man covers two things. First, they must die. This is a matter of comfort to the godly person or the Christian. In knowing the plan of God, that to be absent from the body is to be present with the Lord. That is comfort. It's real.

Secondly, as much as it's a matter of comfort for the Christian, death is a matter of terror to the wicked, for after death comes the judgment! It's an unchangeable decree of God concerning man. They must die. They must be judged. It's easy for folks to agree to the first part of our text today, but few want to admit that judgment follows death.

As we look at this verse we realize that there are similarities between our appointments and God's. The appointments that we set up for ourselves, we have time to prepare for.

Is man more considerate than God? God is just. He gives every man an opportunity to prepare for his appointment. Some men are startled when judgment is mentioned because they haven't prepared for it. There are millions who would be lost if they would die today! Not because they didn't know, but because they have put off accepting Christ.

Why do we preach? Because we want to make folks realize the risk they are taking. 2 Corinthians 5:11 says, "Knowing the terror of the Lord, we persuade men." If you knew that you would be in your coffin tomorrow, you wouldn't sleep tonight. You would be getting ready to meet God: the God that you've forgotten, the God that you've rejected—if you only knew!

That's why we need to prepare *today*.

The Prayers of the Prodigal

In the 15th Chapter of Luke, Jesus presents three parables. In each there is a story of lost and found: the lost sheep, the lost coin and the lost son. When something or someone is lost they need to be found. Jesus came for that purpose—to seek and to save the lost. Luke shows Him as the Seeking Savior. The shepherd went out into the wilderness to find the lost sheep, the woman turned on all of the lights and searched diligently till she found the coin—but in the case of the lost son, the Father waited for the boy to come to himself—to turn towards him in response to the love of the father that reached out over the miles. He said, "I will arise and go to my father." He knew the father's love would receive him—for God so loved the world.

Each story ends with a happy ending, each one starts with a mistake, a wrong turn, a bad decision. As we look at this third parable today I want to focus on the two prayers, or the two requests, that the son made. The first was: *give me*. Verse 12 says, "Father, *give me*, give me the portion of goods that is mine!" It's mine by inheritance and I want it now. We pray *give me* prayers perhaps too often. Dad, *give me* so that I may have a good time; and a good time he had. He wasted his substance in riotous living. Then, sadder and wiser, he prayed a second prayer: *make me.* Thank God it led him home.

We live in a day when too many think of what they can get. Christians have developed the attitude that God owes them something. He owes us health and profit, he owes us guardian angels and protection, and too often they use it wrongfully and expect God to chalk it off to experience without consequences. The *gimme gimme* Christian life always leads to shipwreck. I don't know when the boy woke up to what he had become. Perhaps when he woke up one morning and was eyeball to eyeball to a hog. The road to these hog pens that are owned by citizens are well lighted and highly recommended. You get the feeling that you haven't lived until you taste the good life. You don't have to look hard to find these Hog Heavens. You reach for more and get less and less. There's no satisfaction.

That's why the second prayer of the prodigal is so beautiful. "Father, I have sinned…*make me."* That prayer starts all of Heaven in motion towards you.

That change of attitude and direction starts the restoration process rolling. Repentance must come before salvation. You must come to the place where you say: I am wrong; Father I have sinned; I'm the one who is in trouble; I thought that God owed me something, but now I know that I owe Him everything; I have an obligation to my creator to live my life in His service. Father, make me, melt me, mold me and fill me. You'll get much better treatment as a servant than you did as a rebel.

"The wages of sin is death. The Gift of God is Eternal Life," Romans 6:23. Food is better than famine. Love is better than loneliness. Laughter is better than misery. Forgiveness is sweet music. A robe is far better than rags. The Father can handle your life if you'll let Him.

The God of All Comfort

X-rays and CAT scans are wonderful inventions. Lives have been saved because of them, but there's a kind of heart trouble that technology can't reveal. There's a turbulence inside of many that only Heaven's comfort can fix. Jesus knew that as He headed toward the Cross! He was hated; a price had been paid for His life. He knew that His hour was near. John 12:23, "The hour is come!" and He was ready. The following two chapters were written to help you and I get ready. Jesus was thinking of His men and He wanted to comfort them.

There are seven different reasons for comfort here in John 14 and they're written for us.

The Comfort of Faith—You believe in God. That's all you need to sustain you: Faith in God. You're anchored in Someone! You believe in God? Then trust God's bridge to mankind. Let your faith rest in Jesus. He keeps His Word, "I came once, and I'm coming back!"

The Comfort of Hope—The Father's House is our forwarding address. When the flesh and blood leader tries to offer you the future, be careful. But when the Architect of the Universe offers you a retirement plan, you can count on it! He's preparing a place for us. Revelation 21 is awesome! We prepared a stable for Him—dirt floor, straw, animal smells; He's preparing a *mansion* for us!

The Comfort of His return—Jesus' words John 14:3, "I will come and receive you unto myself!" Man looks for a solution, for a remedy, for a "man" to come with the answers. The Man is coming. He will come again, and not through the world systems. They're not expecting Him. That's why they despise the believer.

The Comfort of Knowing the Way—Jesus gave directions. Have you ever asked directions and couldn't understand them? It's hard sometimes when you're traveling to get there by the directions people give. The way to Heaven can't be misunderstood. Jesus said to Thomas, "I am the Way". Every other way is the wrong way!

The Comfort of a vision or a revelation that God brings—Thomas asked the question, "What is God like?" I love the answer that Jesus gave, "God is just like I am". God loves children. God understands the trials of a housewife in the kitchen. He knows we have tax problems. God appreciates our giving. God heals sick people. God respects marriage. God knows that we need vacations. God helps us solve our problems when we ask Him. "If you've seen me, you've seen the Father."

The Comfort of Prayer—Free long-distance service as often as you want and talk as long as you like. Direct dialing 24 hours a day. There's a privilege that no world system can provide. It's called communion, not only communication. I fellowship with Him while I wait for Him to return.

The Comfort of the Holy Spirit—John 14:16-17. What a tremendous bonus. What comfort. Do you feel like an orphan? You don't need to. Are you feeling overwhelmed by the trials, the pressures of the world system? You have a right. The antagonism against the child of God is real. I need direction through a world of deceit. Jesus said, "The Spirit of Truth will guide you".

No need for heart trouble. Our reservations are secure. Our transfer is being worked on right now. The lines are open. Jesus said, " I will come again!"

God Can See

The human eye is an amazing creation. It is a camera that can picture for you the tiniest speck on the laboratory slide as well as the sun shining 93,000,000 miles away. The eye is mentioned 534 times in the Bible

David asked the question in Psalms 94:9, "He that formed the eye, shall He not see?" The answer is obvious. The Creator who gave us this miraculous instrument is well able to see! We forget the fact too often, especially when we're overwhelmed with sorrow and suffering. We need to remind ourselves that God sees!

He sees our tears and longs to wipe them away (Revelation 7:17). He sees our troubles. They come, but He has promised to be an ever present help in times of trouble (Psalm 91:15). And again in Psalm 46:1, "God is our refuge and strength, an ever present help in times of trouble". Each time God sees our troubles, He takes notice. *God **sees** our trials.* I Peter 1:7 reminds us that the trials of our faith are more precious than gold for it's in the trials that we know that God sees and comes to our rescue.

Are you troubled? God wants to solve your problem. I have the authority of His infallible Word to tell you that He longs to solve your problem. Are you poor? God sees your poverty and longs to provide for you. Are you sick? The Great Physician sees your suffering and will bring you relief. He is in the recovery business. The fact that we have many needs gives us an opportunity to draw from the supplies that are available through the God of our Salvation who sees our needs.

Men have made the mistake many times thinking that God couldn't see them. Did Jonah think that he was running away from God and that God didn't see him sneaking aboard the boat, going in exactly the opposite direction that God wanted him to go? God saw the sailors pitching Jonah overboard into the raging sea, and God saw Jonah repenting in the interior of the great fish!

When God was looking for a liberator to take his children away from the lashes of the Egyptian guards

He saw Moses watching his father-in-law's sheep on the hillside. It's beautiful what God told Moses, "I have seen the affliction of my people". God sees the Christian man or woman who is suffering.

When the Midianites were pressing Israel, God saw a young man named Gideon threshing wheat by his father's winepress. God saw in Gideon a heart of courage and valor that even Gideon didn't know that he had. God saw qualities of leadership and generalship—so the angel addressed him "thou mighty man of valor".

The unpenetrating eye of God sees deep into our hearts and thoughts. He knows the thought and intents of our hearts. Are you pressured or distressed today? You have a tremendous option available to you. Your part is easy. You can gain courage from the prophet in II Chronicles 16:9, "The Eyes of the Lord run to and fro throughout all the earth, to show Himself strong in the behalf of them whose heart is perfect toward Him."

God didn't overlook Daniel in the lion's den. He saw the whole scene. He didn't miss seeing Peter in prison needing divine deliverance. God sees the faithful minister and missionary. He sees the widow and her mite and He even sees the earnest Christian layperson in their private prayer closet.

Sin is a barrier between you and God. That barrier can be removed by confessing your sin and forsaking the life of a loser. God will forgive if you repent.

But God

The words "but" and "and" appear many times in the Word of God. These words are called conjunctives. A conjunction is a word that joins together sentences, clauses, phrases, or words. The word "and" is used in sentence structure to emphasize the preceding idea. When you hear the word "and" you expect a further explanation usually in the positive sense. For example, "She is beautiful *and* she has brains."

The word "but", on the other hand, means "on the contrary". It precedes a time of distress or a negative. "I would like to trust God, *but* I don't think I can." "He is a good provider, *but* does not show love for his family", etc.

Most of the time when "but" is used in the Bible it precedes a specific time when God intervened in a hopeless situation. We were the children of wrath, fulfilling the desires of the flesh and heading full speed, pedal to the metal in the wrong direction to our own destruction—But God! God arrests us, and in arresting us proves His love for us in a very tangible way. He made us alive together with Christ by His Grace *and* lifted us to Heavenly places in Christ.

Prior to the new covenant, the Gentiles were excluded from citizenship. They were foreigners to the promises of God. There was no hope for them, *but* God stepped in *and* now in Christ Jesus the wall of separation has been broken down. It is abolished. We are now reconciled to God through this sacrificial act of God through Jesus Christ, *and* He brought to us peace that passes understanding. Jesus was teaching His disciples concerning those who have their priorities wrong; those who relied on their wealth as their security. In response to His statement about the eye of a needle they were astonished and asked the question, "Who then can be saved?" Jesus looked at them and said, "With men this is impossible, *but* with God all things are possible!" The word "possible" is from the Greek word *dunatos* which means "the ability to act and the power to accomplish". In other words, no matter how powerless we are in our own effort to make things happen, He can demonstrate the dynamic power to translate people from Satan's realm to Gods' kingdom. With God all things are possible.

Remember: *But God* who is rich in mercy is reaching out to you today to make of you what He planned for you to be.

God Forgives and Forgets

The Word of God is full of forgiveness. The facts can't be ignored. Man sinned and came short of the Glory of God (Romans 3:23) far short of His purpose for us to be here, but God in His Mercy provided a way out—an escape from the penalty of sin (Romans 6:23) "He gives life instead of death by Christ Jesus". In Isaiah 43:24 we see that the charge is serious! God says, "Thou hast wearied me with thine iniquities". In other words I'm sick and tired of your sinning—I've had it with man's rebellion.

You would expect Isaiah 43:25 to say, "I even I will destroy thee, I am He that will not be bothered with you any more." If we were dealing with mere man it would possibly have been recorded that way. God has never been able to tolerate sin. That's why He covered Adam and Eve. That's why He turned his back on the cross as Jesus took on Himself the sins of the world. God loves the sinner, but He hates sin. One of the most beautiful words in our language is the word *pardon*. Pardon is the remission of a sentence and forgiving an offense, and the offender. That's why I love Isaiah 43:25, "I will blot out thy transgressions for mine own sake". I'll wipe the slate clean for you. Psalm 103:3 says, "Who forgiveth all thy iniquities?" No matter how far you've gone His mercy and forgiveness will reach you. I John 1:9, "If we confess our sins He will forgive and cleanse". You'll be justified (just as if you'd never sinned). There's no doubt about it—God forgives. Just as light dispels darkness and the sun burns away the fog, He forgives and then He forgets. Isaiah 43:25 says, "I will not remember thy sins".

Satan doesn't let it lie—but God forgets. Jesus forgave Peter at the fire. He forgave His tormentors from the cross. He forgave the thief on the cross. He's in business to forgive. He came to seek and to save the lost. His purpose for coming is recorded in Isaiah 61:1. As you read it apply it to yourself. Jesus turned with compassion and forgave Peter.

He'll forgive you today if you let him.

Close Is Not Enough

Jesus often taught in parables. The root word in the Greek for parable is *paraballo,* or "putting things side by side". Parables are a form of teaching which present the listener with interesting illustrations that emphasize a moral or a religious truth. A parable can illustrate one or more truths. A parable can jolt an audience into seeing things from a different or new point of view. When the Word of God is taught or preached in any form it's purpose is to bring believers to a closer relationship to Jesus, and to bring the unbeliever to a point of commitment. The Word of God affects change. You're never quite the same after a preaching or teaching session than you were prior to it. Hopefully you are better and closer to God, but sad to say, quite often people move in the other direction. They resent the truth of the Word and their heart becomes a little harder.

Man does not want to hear from God. In the longsuffering Mercy of God, He didn't give up on them. He sent His Son (Mark 12:6), "Having therefore one Son". His well beloved. He sent Him—and the ingratitude of these caretakers of God's property became out of control. "Let's kill Him, and get rid of Him. We can take over," they said. Those who heard these words had no idea that in just a few short days they would be screaming, "Crucify Him! Kill Him! Give us Barabbas!" Jesus was hitting home with His parable and they didn't like it. In Mark 12:10 Jesus quoted an Old Testament Scripture that they knew, Psalms 118:22, "The rejected stone became the Cornerstone."

When Jesus is the main message in our churches we'll see them grow. We need to preach and teach Jesus. Our children need to hear that name, they need to be familiar with His story, so that when they are leaders in the church the message will still be the same.

The bottom line is this; love God with every thing that you have! When you love God with all of your heart, then anything that rivals God will be taken off of the throne. Anything that comes between you and God will be gotten rid of—any of the worldly ways that would hang on will fall off if you follow this commandment. If you really believe He is Lord—not one of many, or even one of two, but the Lord is One Lord—then He will have Lordship over the throne of your life. God does not demand our divided attention.

He gives *us* His undivided attention. All of Heaven is at our disposal when we are born into His family, there's nothing that we have to go through alone again. We are more than conquerors when we know Him. All the hosts of hell march out—double time—at the mention of His name. Every promise in the Book is mine. And what does He ask in return? Just that we love Him with all our heart, soul, mind and strength. In considering what we receive in return, that's not much to ask.

Asleep On Death Row

The story in Acts 12: 1-16 took place 11 years after the crucifixion of Christ and His Resurrection. Herod was in charge. Herod ruled the roost. This was Herod, the son of Herod who had the children murdered endeavoring to protect his throne from this Baby that was born King of the Jews. Herod had built the temple: a beauty of gold and marble. It took 46 years of labor. He also built a prison for his enemies. The walls were 20 feet thick. Some of the stones were 30 feet long. It was definitely a maximum-security facility. To enter you went through a massive gate made of iron. There were four of his best soldiers guarding the gate. The second entrance was of huge planks studded with iron bolts. Four more guards stood there. A third gate, again guarded by four men, and as you progressed deep into the prison you came to the inmost cell. The prisoner was chained to two keepers. He couldn't move without alerting the guards—and one prisoner was special! An apostle of Jesus Christ, Peter, the big fisherman, was set to be executed as soon as the Jewish Passover and the Roman pagan holiday called Easter was past. Herod had planned to execute Peter for preaching salvation through faith in a crucified, risen Savior. That was his plan, but Heaven had other plans.

Have you ever been to an all-night prayer meeting? They had one at the home of Mary, John Mark's mother. They employed a young woman, a domestic named Rhoda, who plays a very important role in this story. Herod may have gates of iron and armed guards, but they can't keep out angels! Do you know that angels can speak any language? The angel spoke to Peter in Hebrew, Acts 12: 7 &8. The guards didn't even wake up. These they were chained to nothing and no one. The gates opened on their own. The same power that rolled away the stone from the tomb opened the gates of Herod's prison. God's authority is limitless!

Things weren't going too well at the all-night prayer meeting. Only one of them had faith! It was Rhoda. She was waiting at the door! No one believed her when she reported that Peter was there. She was in a room full of doubt (when in doubt you need a faith lift!). You're seeing things Rhoda. It must be a ghost or Peter's guardian angel. Get a life Rhoda!

What can we learn from this Bible lesson? *Faith in God can save a lot of worry or anxiety!* Jesus saves, Jesus keeps! The soldiers thought that they were the keepers, but Jesus keeps! Jesus is my keeper and my friend!

God hears and answers prayers for temporal as well as spiritual blessings. Verse 5, "Prayer was made without ceasing unto God for him". You're talking Power in corporate prayer of the church. You cannot measure the power of prayer!

There is a difference between the prayer of faith and formal prayers. A difference between saying some prayers and praying through! Rhoda had faith. She was waiting at the door. She expected an answer.

The enemy cannot destroy you when you commit yourself to Jesus. Satan binds you. There is the bondage of habits: habits that you can't afford and are killing you. God can unbind you. He can open the doors.

I've got Good News. He's sending for you now! Start with prayer. Someone cares for you today! Someone is praying for your release! Let Christ light up your dungeon today! Hurry up. Head for the light. Don't stay in prison one minute longer—and then tell somebody!

Who Do Atheists Thank?

In 1966 during the "God is dead" movement, Jim Bishop wrote an article for the Miami Herald titled, "There Is No God?" What Mr. Bishop wrote was written to expose the foolishness of the theory of evolution. The Big Bang people have more faith than believers in what they believe. There is no God? Not hardly!

God formed creation with a design that is eternal. This Great God so loved that He gave His only begotten Son that whosoever will believe in Him should not perish but have eternal life! Everything I am or I have comes from Him. Am I not supposed to be thankful for His provision, for His faithfulness, for His Grace and Mercy, His Peace, and His Comfort in the storm? I must thank Him many times a day with a song of praise. I should and I must praise Him!

The more I live, the more I see how much I have to be thankful for. Let's list a few to help you enjoy your week a little more: I'm thankful for health, family, and many friends, for peace, joy and hope! I'm thankful Lord for the wonders of Your fabulous Creation. I'm thankful that we don't live in the "good old days", before penicillin and heart surgery, and before the cure for polio and tuberculosis. Back then life expectancy was about one-half of what it is today. I don't want to go back to travel by horse and buggy or camel or chariot. To go from here to California would take a season: now it's about 4 ½ to 5 hours. I'm glad we're able to explore space and view galaxies through giant telescopes. I hear people grumbling about the lack of speed of a Pentium II or III. How would you like to communicate by smoke signals or drums or homing pigeons?

I'm thankful for friends. It's a really poor man, no matter what he has in assets, if he has no friends. We all need voices of encouragement, remembering birthdays, sharing laughs and sorrows, phone calls at just the right time, visits when we're sick and prayer when we're hurting. I'm thankful for spiritual blessings: the Gift of salvation—something we could never earn. I'm thankful for the infilling of the Holy Spirit that gives Power to be a witness and Power for Holy living, and The Word which guides us on our journey. Lord, I thank you for your plan that fulfills the soul of man—healing our mortal bodies and healing of our never dying souls and for filling our cup to overflowing.

I'm thankful for hope. Hope in life through the Lord Jesus. Thankful for the ability to be an overcomer through Faith in God's Word. I find Hope in verses like Philippians 4:13, "I can do all things through Christ who strengthens me". We are not slaves to environment or heredity or circumstances. What about the Hope of Eternal Life? Not only eternal but meaningful and fulfilling. Thank you for the hope of seeing mom and dad, and loved ones who've gone ahead.

I thank God for freedom: freedom in Christ, freedom from guilt and sin and bondage, freedom from tyranny and oppression, and freedom from being arrested for our faith. I'm thankful for the joy of living in the land of the free and the home of the brave. Freedom of speech is precious, as is freedom to worship without interference, to own and study the Word of God freely.

What are you thankful for this week? Take inventory today and give God thanks!

Why I Am An Optimist

In today's world there are lots of reasons to be a pessimist. Look at the headlines just from this week. The Middle East is in turmoil. People die somewhere on this planet on a daily basis for their pet causes with no noticeable results. South Africa is about to experience civil war. Indonesia is in turmoil. The drug trade is in turmoil. The drug trade is out of control. Gas prices are going through the roof. In China one billion people are flexing their muscles as the world watches in fear. On the health scene, cancer is still coming on strong. AIDS is out of control and no one seems to care. Men's hearts fail for a catalog of reasons. Death by drunk drivers takes more lives per year that the entire Viet Nam war. The world is desperately sick. So it seems there are a lot of reasons to be a pessimist! But the real Christian can genuinely be optimistic. We don't have to fall to the contagious pessimism.

It's not a new thing. Here's a little history lesson: Back in the 18th Century William Pitt was ready to hang it up, "There is scarcely anything around us but ruin and despair." A century later William Wilberforce despaired, "I dare not marry, the future is too dark." In 1849 Disraeli cried out, "In industry, commerce and agriculture there is not hope." Let's go back a little farther—back to the Roman Empire days. How would you have liked to live under the oppression of Rome? In normal times, emperors like Caligula and Nero would have been committed to an insane asylum. They were real lunatics.

Against the backdrop of filth and corrosion, violence and godlessness, rose the world's most magnificent and awesome figure: A Carpenter form Nazareth who said "Be of Good Cheer" (John 16:33). This messenger of Hope was Jesus Christ. The Anointed Son of God, Jesus was an avowed optimist. He was realistic. He understood the times, the degradation and the corruption, yet He was so Powerful that when He came to this planet, He shook the gates of hell off their hinges! That's why we can sing, "My hope is built on nothing less than Jesus' Blood and Righteousness, on Christ the Solid Rock I stand!" What was it that gave Jesus the optimism that He displayed while He walked this sod? John's Gospel begins with a reason for optimism, "In the beginning was the Word" (John 1:1) and the Word was Jesus Himself!

I can have optimism because He is in control. You know the lyrics, "He's got the whole world in His hands"! No wonder He could say, "Be of Good cheer, I have overcome the world!" (John 16:33)

Being an optimist does not do away with reality. There are hardships in life, no doubt. Tragedy and suffering are real. There is disease and there is death. Sorrow and crying are close by. No one hated sin as much as Jesus did, and no one loved the sinner as deeply as Jesus did!

How about you? What could Jesus do in your life if you gave yourself to Him totally? We almost become practical atheists when we have a pessimistic attitude and lifestyle.

Paul was an optimist. In a dungeon under Nero's palace, waiting for the executor Paul wrote, "Rejoice in the Lord always. Again I say rejoice!" (Philippians 4:4) Paul was an optimist because he followed the Lord!

Accountability

There are several things that are more important than ability: availability, stability, and accountability. Every believer is responsible for their own actions. We are responsible for the type of building that we build, individually and as parents we are responsible for the material we use in building our children.

We have been given a perfect foundation—His name is Jesus. In Christ we have all that we need to overcome and to live an abundant life—we cannot shirk our responsibility. Everyone must give an account of himself to God. Not the pastor, or the priest, or the rabbi, or Mom, or Dad. To God Himself we must give an accounting of our life.

Please remember that God is a God of perfect love and perfect justice. In our culture we don't see perfect justice, or any justice at all sometimes. Our systems are plagued with problems and shortcomings. Guilty men are let go because of some technicality, and innocent men are locked up because of poor defense or circumstances that went against them, prejudices or false witnesses, etc. *Where is justice?* But God has perfect Justice, and we are inexcusable before Him.

You are accountable to God in two areas: for your salvation and for your choices. You are not what you wish but what you choose. God has made life available to us through Christ and we must make the right choice. Choose life today for He will not hold you guiltless if you reject, or neglect, so great a Salvation.

God has not left us as orphans without help or power. He has given us equipment: tools to build with. One great asset to our accountability is our conscience, that still small voice within us that gives us many signals that warn us of error and lead us to truth. That steers us to the best building material. This guidance can be violated when we refuse to listen to those inner warnings.

Let's get our focus on Jesus and learn to live as He showed us! He is the Perfect One—who doesn't fail! You are accountable to be the best you that you can be for God.

The true measure is God's Standard. When we see ourselves in His eyes we realize that our complete dependence is on His keeping power.

Let God direct you in your priorities and choices.

Advice to the Captives

This world is full of people who have been beaten down. People who are captives in their thoughts: thinking that no one cares anymore. They feel alone and useless. The teachers of humanism have told them that they are animals—and they believe it! Dreams are gone. The sparkle of life has disappeared and tomorrow doesn't excite them. The reasons are many and varied: a deep hurt, the loss of a job, the loss of a loved one, financial worries. The world has said, "You're through!"

C.H. Spurgeon has stated that, "The greatest Power in my life has not come through the *mountain tops,* but through the *valleys*. I have learned how to survive and to overcome through afflictions! Look at Moses—his career fell apart when he was 40 years of age. By the time he was 80 he was herding sheep in North Africa, around him nothing but sand, rocks and desolation. But God hadn't given up on him. God had big plans for Moses and before long his name was a household word in Egypt. Three million people would owe their very lives to him! God turned loss into gain—He turned defeat in victory!

God said through Jeremiah (verse 29:11) to the captives, "I know my thoughts toward you! Thoughts of peace and not of evil!" The world said that Moses was a loser. God said, "He's a winner!" The public had written these captives off, but God had a different opinion and no one can change God's opinion about a person (except that person).

God knows your value. There is no promotional company that can raise you in Gods' sight—not even Madison Avenue's best—and there's no committee or council or media or gossip in your town that can drag your name down before Him! When will we learn that God is sovereign? God is the last and final word, and He sees the end from the beginning—believe it or not—even that which seems evil is designed, by God, for Good!

When you give yourself to Jesus Christ and allow Him to be your Savior, you become the property of God. When God stops your funeral procession and gives you new life through the Resurrection Power of Jesus you become His possession And God takes good care of His property! God considers you a valuable commodity. He is crazy about you; you are worth His time and investment. It was a tremendous price and no one can change His mind. He made you. He redeemed you. He made you, like you are, for a reason and GOD DOESN'T MAKE JUNK. God has a plan for you but He will not insist on it against your will. You are not a robot! You can choose to lose but I want you to know that all Heaven wants you to win!

Lift up your eyes to Jesus right now. The angels are watching. Heaven is focusing on you. Softly and tenderly Jesus is calling!

An Outstretched Hand

In Stockholm, Sweden, several years ago, a young lady raced toward a streetcar with her arms full of packages. In her hurry to get there she tripped and was pinned under the trolley. People tried to set her free but couldn't. They called for a crane to lift the heavy car from her broken body. She seemed that she was close to going into shock. Suddenly a man pushed through the crowd and crawled under the car as near as he could get to her. He reached out his fingertips to hers and said gently, "Here, take my hand" And she did. That touch, that contact, that concerned person reaching out to her was enough to keep her from going into shock! Later she expressed her gratitude. She said, "I never knew an outstretched hand could mean so much!" What a tremendous spiritual parallel! When man lay bruised, and broken, torn and bleeding by sin and sickness, loaded down with guilt and shame, pressured by worry and fear, God stepped on the scene. Through His Son Jesus Christ, He put Himself on the same level as man and reached out a helping hand. He came down to my level.

Throughout the world, we see the evidence of that precious touch from His compassionate hand. In Mark's Gospel there are many references to His touch that will bless your soul and strengthen your faith today. In Mark 1 Jesus came to Simon's house. Simon (who later was called Peter) and Andrew, his brother, lived with their family in Capernaum. This became Jesus' unofficial headquarters for His three-year earthly ministry. Peter's mother-in-law was sick. In Matthew's record, the writer says that Jesus *noticed* that she was sick, and touched her hand and the fever left her. It was His touch—the touch of the Master's strong hand that means so much. Jesus noticed the need, and He was and *is* more than willing to meet the need.

It's just another proof that He is a true High Priest. Truly the One Mediator between God and man. Earthly priests don't move in the circles that Jesus moved in. You found Him with the broken and the bruised, the drunkard and the crooks, for it was there that His touch was most appreciated. His credentials allow Him to cross denominational barriers, to break down the walls of partition between races, to scale prison walls and set the captive free. He moves freely into hospital rooms and funeral homes. Jesus often visits death row to give eternal pardon to one who in a short time will be executed.

It's not magic; it's the Word of God! Jesus told the lad with the bread and fish, "Bring them to me". He says the same to you and I, "Bring Me your sins, your doubts, your habits, your heavy burdens, and your fears!" As you do that, as you let Him touch you and change you, you'll agree with the girl that was trapped under the car "I never know that an outstretched hand could mean so much."

It's Never Too Late To Change

The "begats", or the genealogies, of the Bible have never been listed as priority reading for me. There is, however, some tremendous inspiration and education hidden there if you only take the time to study. From verse 1 to verse 17 of Matthew I, there are 42 generations of the lineage of Christ. His Roots have been carefully sought out. Several years ago Alex Haley wrote a book called Roots. It became the highest rated TV series in recent history. It's fascinating to learn about your roots. Walking through Matthew I you sense the same intrigue. We're looking at the earthly roots of the family of our Lord and Savior. On December 25 we celebrated His birthday—and what a birthday it was!

His mother was a virgin, Mary of Nazareth. His Father was God. The man who raised Him was a businessman, a carpenter. The genealogy in Matthew I is Joseph's family history. The list includes cowards and heroes, peaceful people and violent people, holy men and women, as well as killers and prostitutes. King David's great, great grandmother ran a house of prostitution in Jericho. It's in the Holy Bible (the Book of Joshua).

Did you notice that David is in this lineup? Verse 6 states: "Jesse begat David and David begat Solomon through an affair with Bathsheba, the wife of Uriah." That's scary! David was guilty of adultery and planned the accidental death of Uriah, his lover's husband. Come on God—David?! Sin with a capital "S" from someone who should have known better. Why didn't God blot him out? Because David had a heart for God!

His heart cry to God is recorded in Psalm 51:1-4 and 7. This is not a prayer of one who was sorry that he was caught. No, it's a prayer of one who knows that he has violated God's trust in him. He disappointed God willfully and he did the right thing. David threw himself on the altar making no excuses.

If you're going to play the blame game you'll get no relief from your conscience. If you really repent, God will blot out your sin and never remember them against you again. God heard David's cry and picked him up. His life was not over. It was just starting! He became Israel's greatest king and part of the lineage of Jesus.

It's not too late for you today. Jesus loves you and has a plan for your life! Get with the plan.

New Beginnings

2 Corinthians 5:17, "Therefore, if any man be in Christ, he is a new creature; old things are passed way; behold, all things are become new."

This verse in Corinthians is one of the most familiar in the New Testament. God offers mankind a brand new start! When you truly become a new creature or a new creation, you start without a mark against you. No religion—no "ism"—no philosophy on earth can offer you a brand new start and follow through. God is in the creating business—and when He creates us anew He calls it Good. Born again is the right term although it's been abused and misused. It still describes what being In Christ can do to a person. Being born again does not necessarily change our circumstances—but it changes the person, our behavior, our nature, our outlook, our goals, our interests, and our reactions. They are all changed, and then we can handle our circumstances. God takes the old and re-creates us to something new.

God began re-creating men way back in the Old Testament days. He still does it today. He's not limited by age or color or creed or social status. You've heard it said, "You can't teach an old dog new tricks" But God can! With man it's impossible, but not with God.

Abraham was 75 years old. He was wealthy. He was a senior citizen: 75 years old. He was doing well in business, and had a nice spread in a place called Ur, the main city of Chaldea. Chaldea was located down around the Persian Gulf. It was a good place to live and die, but God had bigger plans for Abraham than to grow old and pass away. God called him to an adventure that would change the world. God said in Genesis 12:2, "I will make thee a great nation". Abraham didn't wait. At 75 years of age he said, "Let's go for it". He started over. A brand new start…and the rest is history.

"Jesus Christ is the same yesterday today and forever," (Hebrews 13:8). God is still in the "New Beginning" business. He breaks chains, heals hurts, forgets the past, delivers folks from addiction and bondage.

He'll recreate your mind and your heart today if you'll only ask.

Priorities

About a mile and a half east of Jerusalem is the little town of Bethany. There was a home in Bethany that Jesus loved to visit: the home of Lazarus, Mary and Martha. He could always count on a welcome—an open door of friendliness and good Jewish hospitality. It was imperative that He go through Bethany on this day so Jesus took this opportunity to visit His good friends. He was no sooner in the home when Martha began preparing a meal in the kitchen. Just a question. Does Jesus feel at home in your house? Is He a welcome guest? Is the atmosphere in your home conducive for this wonderful guest? It can be! Martha worked and worried, boiled and stirred and all the while she was boiling inside Mary hadn't lifted a hand to help her. She just sat at the feet of Jesus and drank in every word that He said. Martha banged pans and muttered under her breath hoping to get Mary's attention. Finally she blurted out. She looked like Golda from Fiddler on the Roof, storming out of the kitchen—and Jesus stopped her, "Martha, Martha, you worry too much". Mary has chosen something more precious than natural food. In Moffat's translation it says, "Mary has chosen the Good Part." She knew that He was the Bread of Heaven! The Water of Life! Honey in the Rock! Don't get so concerned with the things of life that you don't take time to listen to His Word!

David knew how to choose the Good Part. See Psalm 119:103, "How sweet are Thy words to my mouth. Yea, sweeter than honey to the taste." David read the menu rightly. Job knew also, Job 23:12, "I have esteemed the Words of Thy mouth more than necessary food!" Ezekiel 3: 2-3, "He caused me to eat the scroll…and it was in my mouth as honey for sweetness!" When we taste all of the dishes that our world dishes out, we lose our appetite for the Best Dish.

If you feed on a diet of magazines, novels, and TV for so long that it makes your spiritual stomach shrivel up, you're in trouble. You lose your appetite for the Word of God! The inner man must eat daily. There is life in the Word.